THE POLICY-
MAKING
PROCESS

W9-BZI-122

PRENTICE-HALL FOUNDATIONS OF MODERN POLITICAL SCIENCE SERIES

Robert A. Dahl, Editor

THE AGE OF IDEOLOGY-POLITICAL THOUGHT, 1750 TO THE PRESENT, Second Edition
by Isaac Kramnick and Frederick M. Watkins

THE AMERICAN PARTY SYSTEM AND THE AMERICAN PEOPLE, Second Edition
by Fred I. Greenstein

THE ANALYSIS OF INTERNATIONAL RELATIONS, Second Edition
by Karl W. Deutsch

CONGRESS AND THE PRESIDENCY, Third Edition
by Nelson W. Polsby

DATA ANALYSIS FOR POLITICS AND POLICY
by Edward R. Tufte

MODERN POLITICAL ANALYSIS, Third Edition
by Robert A. Dahl

MODERN POLITICAL ECONOMY
by Norman Frohlich and Joe A. Oppenheimer

NORMATIVE POLITICAL THEORY
by Fred M. Frohock

PERSPECTIVES IN CONSTITUTIONAL LAW, with Revisions
by Charles L. Black, Jr.

THE POLICY-MAKING PROCESS, Second Edition
by Charles E. Lindblom

PUBLIC OPINION
by Robert E. Lane and David O. Sears

PUBLIC ADMINISTRATION (Forthcoming)
by James W. Fesler

PRENTICE-HALL FOUNDATIONS OF MODERN POLITICAL SCIENCE SERIES

Robert A. Dahl, Editor

PRENTICE-HALL, INC., Englewood Cliffs, New Jersey 07632

THE POLICY-
MAKING
PROCESS

Second Edition

Theodore Lownik Library
Illinois Benedictine College
Lisle, Illinois 60532

CHARLES E. LINDBLOM

Yale University

Library of Congress Cataloging in Publication Data

LINDBLOM, CHARLES EDWARD, (date)
 The policy-making process.

 (Prentice-Hall foundations of modern
political science series)
 Bibliography: p. 125
 Includes index.
 1. United States—Politics and Government.
2. Policy sciences. 3. Power (Social sciences)

I. Title.
JK271.L52   1980   320.9'73   79-15539
ISBN 0-13-686543-7

PRENTICE-HALL FOUNDATIONS OF MODERN POLITICAL SCIENCE SERIES

Robert A. Dahl, Editor

THE POLICY-MAKING PROCESS, Second Edition
 by Charles E. Lindblom

© 1980, by PRENTICE-HALL, INC., Englewood Cliffs, New Jersey. All rights reserved. No part

of this book may be reproduced in any form or by any means without permission in writing

from the publisher. Printed in the United States of America.

PRENTICE-HALL INTERNATIONAL, INC., London
PRENTICE-HALL OF AUSTRALIA, PTY. LTD., Sydney
PRENTICE-HALL OF CANADA, LTD., Toronto
PRENTICE-HALL OF INDIA PRIVATE LIMITED, New Delhi
PRENTICE-HALL OF JAPAN, INC., Tokyo
PRENTICE-HALL OF SOUTHEAST ASIA PTE. LTD., Singapore
WHITEHALL BOOKS LIMITED, WELLINGTON, New Zealand

10 9 8 7 6 5 4 3 2 1

TO BENJAMIN AND NICHOLAS

CONTENTS

ACKNOWLEDGEMENTS

For their valuable critiques and suggestions, which substantially altered the book, my thanks to Louise Comfort (San Jose State), David Caputo (Purdue), Robert A. Dahl (Yale), John Donovan (Bowdoin), George Edwards III (Texas A & M), James W. Fesler (Yale), Terrence Jones (U. Missouri), Michael Kraft (U. Wisconsin), Edward Pauly (Yale), and Dennis Rondinelli (Syracuse).

For editorial assistance, my thanks to Richard Smithey. For his meticulous search for and discovery of many hundreds of instances in which a change of word or phrasing would simplify or otherwise clarify, my special thanks to Eric N. Lindblom, at the time an undergraduate. For excellence in typing and preparing the manuscript for publication, I also wish to record my great appreciation to Robin Ellis.

CHAPTER ONE

A POLICY-MAKING VIEW OF POLITICS

In *The Republic,* Plato set out to analyze justice: what it is and how to achieve it. Machiavelli took up the problem of how to win and hold power and Hobbes asked how to maintain law and order in the face of society's tendency to dissolve into "a war of all against all." Rousseau asked, in his monumental sentence, why "man is born free, and everywhere he is in chains." Although all wrote on different aspects of politics, none made policy making his main interest.

Both the French Declaration of the Rights of Man and the American Declaration of Independence ring with words of tyranny, rights, and liberty, but not with words of the policy-making process. Historically, people have turned to democracy primarily as a guarantor of personal liberty, not as a policy-making process nor as a process for popular control of policy making. Indeed, like some of the Constitutional fathers, many feared that popular control of policy making would lead back to tyranny.

One great figure in Western social thought made policy making, particularly its efficiency or rationality, central to his work, beginning an intellectual tradition that persists to this day. In his *Wealth of Nations,* Adam Smith addressed the inefficiencies of contemporary governments' commercial policies. He proposed to take economic policy making as far as possible out of government hands by putting economic affairs under the control of market buying and selling. The study of rationality in public affairs was then adopted by the new profession of economics, which thereafter largely ignored government and instead praised the virtues of the market as an instrument for social rationality. In political science, the study of government policy making and of its rationality remained subordinate to other interests, coming to the forefront only recently. As political scientists now turn with intense interest to questions about policy making, they bring long-neglected elements back into the analysis of political systems. Newcomers to political science not yet acquainted with its established concerns may feel some surprise that the study of policy making only recently has become a main theme in political science.

EFFICACY AND POPULAR CONTROL

In the liberal democratic world, perhaps the two overriding questions asked about governmental policy making focus on its efficacy in solving problems and on its responsiveness to popular control.

The question of efficacy takes various forms: How intelligently does government cope with the nation's problems? Does government know what it is doing? Do political leaders debate policies thoughtfully? Is government perhaps necessarily inefficient? What accounts for its major blunders? What can be done to raise the level of efficacy in policy making? Can social science help? Can experts help? Why are some persistent problems never solved: for example, strikes, care of the mentally infirm, and urban blight.

The question of popular control also comes in many forms. Who really makes policy? Is policy actually made by elites? Does the ordinary citizen have much influence on policy? Could he if he tried? Do elections really matter? Does it matter which party wins? Would more popular participation in government be a good thing? Why, in a professed democracy, does the public appear to tolerate such offenses against itself as inequitable taxes, street violence, corruption in business and government, inadequate medical care for much of the population, poor schools, and inadequate public services?

Exploration of such questions as these will become an analysis of the whole political system. Largely directed at national policy making in the United States, the analysis will give, however, some attention to democratic politics abroad and to some aspects of authoritarian systems. Unlike many of the new books on policy, this analysis will not examine the pros and cons of particular policies— for example, energy or anti-inflation policies. It asks instead how policies are made.

HOW TO STUDY THE PROCESS

To understand who or what makes policy, one must understand the characteristics of the participants, what parts or roles they play, what authority and other powers they hold, and how they deal with and control each other. Of many different kinds of participants, each plays a specialized role: ordinary citizens, interest-group leaders, legislators, legislative leaders, party activists, party leaders, judges, civil servants, technical experts, and businessmanagers.

What is the best way to learn the intricacies of policy making? A popular method in recent years separates policy making into its component steps and analyzes each step in turn. One studies first how policy problems arise and appear on the agenda of government decision makers, then how people formulate issues for action, next how legislative or other action follows, how administrators subsequently implement the policy, and finally at the end of the process, how policy is evaluated.[1]

One quickly discovers, however, that the cast of characters in this drama does not change greatly in moving from the first act to the last. Moreover, the ways in which they cooperate or struggle with each other do not vary greatly from one step to another. Certain intellectual issues or puzzles also run through every act or step. Our approach, for the most part, organizes the analysis around those aspects of policy making common to all the steps. A predominantly step-by-step analysis of policy making might obscure universal issues and phenomena in searching for those aspects of policy making unique to each step. We do, however, look into certain special problems of setting the agenda, as well as those of implementation.

The Limited Competence of Political Science

Our approach has the additional advantage of permitting us to focus on matters on which political science has something to offer. It does not require us to move, step by step, through explanations on which ordinary knowledge will serve just as well. Social scientists need to guard against explaining what people already know.

Take, for example, the first step in the above hypothetical sequence: building the policy agenda. Many observations can be made: among others, that the discontent of politically inactive citizens will not put their problem on the policy-making agenda; that in addition some activist, perhaps an interest-group leader or a candidate for office, must raise the issue so as to bring it to the attention of officials; that some participants in politics enjoy easy access to policy-making officials and others do not; and that some members of the bureaucracy play an important role in calling problems to the attention of official policy makers. Such a list can be made by any reasonably informed and thoughtful person. Most peo-

---

[1]Different authors see the sequence in slightly different ways. Harold Lasswell, one of the principal originators of this approach, laid out the following steps: intelligence, recommending, prescribing, invoking, applying, appraising, and terminating (H. Lasswell, "The Public Interest," in *The Public Interest,* ed. C. F. Friedrich [*Nomos,* vol. 5] New York: Atherton Press, 1962).

ple, even poets and ballet dancers, know a great deal about this and other aspects of policy making.[2]

Political science offers illuminating propositions on only some few of the many aspects of determination of the agenda. One, for example, is that social learning or indoctrination creates a climate of opinion that keeps many issues, especially issues challenging the fundamentals of the political-economic system itself, off the agenda. For example, most of us have learned to believe in a two-house Congress, and we therefore do not seriously consider abolishing the Senate. A second is that agendas are in large part determined by interaction among persons struggling with each other over the terms of their cooperation. Most policy problems seem to arise out of this cooperation. The existence of government opens up opportunities for cooperative action—to dam rivers, to educate the young, to fly to the moon—that otherwise would be impossible. How then can these opportunities be exploited, who should exploit them, and to whose advantage? All these complicated issues become part of the policy agenda.

Policy Making as an Untidy Process

The step-by-step approach also risks falling into an assumption that policy making proceeds through a relatively orderly, rationalistic process, like writing a term paper with a beginning, a middle, and an end, with each part tied logically to each succeeding part. That policy making proceeds in this manner should be questioned rather than assumed.

Some features of policy making argue sharply against such an assumption. For example, one group's solution becomes another group's problem. High farm prices solve the farmers' problem but create a problem for consumers. In addition, a host of policy problems comes onto the agenda as a result of attempts to implement other policies. Consequently, the step called implementation and the step called agenda-building collapse into each other. The United States, for example, needs policies to curb the Central Intelligence Agency and other intelligence agencies largely because of prior decisions to use these agencies to implement national security policy. From the seedbed of implementation, new policy problems grow and are plucked for the agenda.[3]

Notice also that policy evaluation, often regarded as the end-of-the-

---

[2]For that reason, we have not taken up a page or two with definitions of policy and policy making. Almost any definition will do, except those limiting "policy" to decisions about standing rules to be imposed on decision making, as in: "It is the senator's policy to take an active part in all farm legislation." That is too narrow a concept. For our purpose, a standing decision is indeed a policy decision, but so are many ensuing specific decisions taken on farm legislation.

[3]See the chapter "Policy As Its Own Cause," in Aaron Wildavsky, *Speaking Truth to Power: The Art and Craft of Policy Analysis* (Boston: Little, Brown & Co., 1979).

line last step, does not constitute a step in policy *making* unless it throws light on possible next moves in policy. If a distinctive step at all, policy evaluation becomes intertwined with all other attempts to appraise and formulate possible next moves in policy.

Moreover, a policy sometimes is formed from a political compromise among policy makers, none of whom had in mind quite the problem to which the agreed policy responds. Sometimes, as we have just noted, policies spring from new opportunities, not from "problems" at all. We can say that policy in the United States government leaves broad scope for business monopoly, especially in the form of oligopoly, thus restricting prosecution under antitrust law to no more than a small number of cases. No official or agency so decided. The policy emerges somehow from the policy-making system but not by orderly steps.

We will look at policy making as an extremely complex process without beginning or end and whose boundaries remain most uncertain. Somehow a complex set of forces together produces effects called "policies." As already noted, one can look at all of government and politics as a policy-making process. Doing so, one will not fall into the error of subsuming policy making as one aspect of politics, as when analyzed as a sequence of steps. Thoughtful people sometimes despair of fixing responsibility on any official or body for the failures of policy making. They find it difficult even to grasp the multiplicity of influences bearing on policy. Their frustrations might be said to prove our point: to understand policy making one must understand all of political life and activity.

EVALUATION OF THE POLICY-MAKING PROCESS

Once described, can we evaluate the policy-making process? To some, the slow process of racial desegregation in American schools—a desegregation still incomplete decades after the Supreme Court decision ordering it—is conclusive evidence of defects in American policy making. Yet if desegregation moves slowly because of policy-making sensitivity to democratically expressed public opinion, can one call the process defective?

The difficulties of evaluation often are vivid. Did President Truman's order for the atomic bombing of Japan reveal a scandalous flaw in American policy making or a moment of admirable decisiveness? Did President Kennedy's gamble on atomic war in the Cuban missile crisis demonstrate the capacity of American policy making to rise to heights of rational calculation or its indefensible reliance on the too hasty consultations of too few officials (even though his handling of the issue did not provoke a nuclear war)? Did congressional and judicial decision making measure up to the task of coping with Watergate's challenges to a democratic society, as some observers claim, or was the nation saved from the consequences of conspiracy by the accident of President Nixon's taping the evidence against himself?

The difficulties of evaluating the policy-making process do not turn simply on the inconclusiveness of evaluations of specific policies or episodes. As already noted, most people want policy making generally to be democratic. But they also want it to be intelligent. The two criteria call for contradictory features in policy making. We cannot even specify what we mean by democratic policy making. For example, does British prime ministerial policy making come closer to democracy than presidential-congressional policy making does? Does a high level of interest-group influence on policy come closer than a low level?

That the evaluation is difficult and inconclusive does not argue against attempting it. But the clarification of fundamental facts about policy making is a task that precedes evaluation. That we can do within the confines of this small book while evaluation we cannot.

POLICY MAKING AND POLICY OUTPUTS

Policies and policy outputs differ in democratic and authoritarian systems. Authoritarian systems, for example, do not pursue policies designed to protect civil liberties. Nor do all authoritarian systems ensure the conventional rights of private property. Democratic systems always have. In principle, a democratic system could end all private ownership of productive assets and establish in its place a system of production directed by the government. That no democratic nation has even tried to do so stands as a remarkable historical fact.[4]

Some other differences between democratic and authoritarian outputs remain to be discovered, just as do some differences among the outputs of various kinds of democratic policy making. But the discovery that in many policy areas differences among policy-making systems do not make much difference in outputs has jarred political science. As between the democratic and communist systems in Europe that are at similar levels of economic development, for example, public expenditures for education and welfare programs are much alike.[5]

A number of political scientists have been comparing policy making in the American states. They try to measure the degree to which differences in educational, welfare, and highway programs, among others,

---

[4]For a controversial view of the relation between democracy and private property, see William Kingston, "The Lemmings of Democracy," *Studies,* 65 (Winter 1976). See also Charles E. Lindblom, *Politics and Markets* (New York: Basic Books, 1977), chapter 12.
    [5]Frederick L. Pryor, *Public Expenditures in Communist and Capitalist Nations* (Homewood, Ill.: Richard D. Irwin, 1968), especially p. 310.

depend on policy-making differences among the states, such as in degree of party competition, systems of representation, strength of the governor's office, and voter turnout. Apparently these differences in the political system matter less to policy outputs than earlier assumed. Such socioeconomic factors as the wealth of the state and its degree of industrialization count more heavily.

At this stage in the research, one cannot confidently make stable generalizations about which differences in the policy-making system result in significant differences in policy output. The picture is complicated by the finding that some socioeconomic differences among the states produce differences in methods of policy making, rather than directly resulting in differences in outputs. Nevertheless, this rich new research undercuts many older professional views that confidently alleged that the policy-making system matters greatly to policy output. It also suggests that the reform of policy making may not greatly improve outputs.[6]

All over the world, either dominant elites or masses appear to want, among other things, law and order, agricultural and industrial production, and mobility and communication. If, through such accomplishments as these, they think they can afford others, they then want increasingly productive technologies, minimum standards of living for almost everyone, and new ventures in research, education, and exploration. These ambitions, not the policy-making process, explain why governments pursue the policies or outputs they do. The policy-making process can explain partially how governments pursue their various policy targets, but not why the targets are chosen.

---

[6]The research includes contributions by Cnudde, Cutright, Dawson, Dye, Grumm, Hofferbert, McCrone, Robinson, and Sharkansky, among others. It is summarized and analyzed in Richard I. Hofferbert, *The Study of Public Policy* (Indianapolis: Bobbs-Merrill, 1974), chapters 4–6.

PART ONE

INFORMATION AND ANALYSIS IN POLICY MAKING

CHAPTER TWO

ANALYSIS
IN
POLICY MAKING

The preceding chapter identified two overriding questions about the policy-making process: how to make policies more effective in actually solving social problems, and how to make policy making responsive to popular control. On the first question, perhaps most people believe that the answer lies in bringing more information, thought, and analysis into the policy-making process. Reflecting the recent and rising concern with the first question, the study of policy making has paid special attention to the roles of information and analysis in the policy-making process. Some books and courses focus almost entirely on these intellectual components of policy making.

In the face of social problems now seeming to threaten human survival—energy shortage, environmental degradation, and atomic war, for example—demands for more informed and more carefully analyzed policies have become all the more intense. These new demands for analysis often mix with some anxieties about who can be trusted to do the analyzing. Would one believe a public utility company's analysis of the need for nuclear generation of electric power? The demands also sometimes clash with the frequent antirationalist sentiment of recent years, a sentiment declaring that intellectual approaches to problems often miss the point in their preoccupation with statistics and bloodless analytical categories. Nevertheless, the demand for more information and analysis seems unmistakable. And it calls in particular for a reduction of the partisan political conflict often standing in the way of analysis.

Yet the second of the two questions—the one about popular control —requires that to some important degree, policy making remain forever political. Very few people in democratic societies wish to go so far as to surrender their own political roles and interests in policy making. Most of them want to vote at least in some elections. Most also want to be able to tell their representatives their opinions on various issues, even if as ordinary citizens they do not qualify as experts on the issues. And although people believe that governments need more research and analysis on policy problems, they apparently intend that their elected officials remain in charge. Officials, they believe, should call on the services of analysts and experts but not abdicate their political functions to them.

In short, a deep conflict runs through common attitudes toward policy making. On the one hand, people want policy to be informed and well analyzed. On the other hand, they want policy making to be democratic, hence necessarily political. In slightly different words, on the one hand they want policy making to be more scientific; on the other, they want it to remain in the world of politics.[1]

Many democratic theorists and political leaders have tried to resolve the conflict. They assure us that open political interchange in a democratic society—a "competition of ideas"—is the best road to truth, that democratic politics after all offers the best chance for informed and reasoned policy making. But we cannot be sure. Even if the best road, it looks perilous. Many people distrust democratic politics because they believe that the competition of ideas brings less reason than contentiousness into policy making. And so the conflict between reason, analysis, and science on the one side, and politics and democracy on the other, remains. If a society wants more reason and analysis in policy making, perhaps it must surrender some aspects of democracy.

Yet although these two main components of policy making—analysis and politics—conflict with each other, they also in some ways can complement each other. On some issues, for example, a legislator's constituents might be pleased to let his or her legislative vote be decided by a careful study of the issues rather than by the influence of their uninformed wishes. Perhaps then, despite the conflict, a society can enjoy both reasoned and democratic policy making, or at least make some improvement on both fronts.

Thus we pose a central theme for the entire book: the conflict between analysis and politics in policy making and the possibilities that

[1]Of course, all governmental policy making is political in one sense of "political." But we shall use the term "political" more narrowly so that we can contrast analysis and politics in policy making, even though in the other broader sense both are political. The distinction could be put as one between reaching policy choices by information and analysis, on one hand, or by exerting power, on the other. It also could be put as one between choosing policies by informed and thoughtful analysis and discussion, on one hand, and by elections, bargaining, trading of favors, and wheeling and dealing on the other. For example, analysis appears prominently in decisions of the Federal Reserve Board on monetary policy; politics appear prominently in congressional decisions on the location of military bases in the various states. Analysis and politics always intertwine.

the two, at least in some ways, can complement each other. The conflict poses great difficulties in the United States, as in every society.

We shall begin our investigation of the policy-making process by looking first at analysis in policy making: how practiced in government, its potential, and its difficulties.[2] We then shall move into the political elements in policy making, as well as into the intricate connections between the analysis and politics.

THE UBIQUITY OF ANALYSIS

How far do facts, reason, rational discussion, and analysis go in policy making? In all political systems people gather facts, analyze them, and debate issues. Although these activities are often hurried and the results challenged or actually discarded, they are never absent. We need to appreciate their scope before investigating the frequency with which they are pushed aside.

Public officials, journalists, interest-group leaders, and interested citizens often join in informed discussion. In wealthy countries like the United States, specialized professional fact-finding, research, and policy analyses flourish as routine inputs into policy making. A policy maker will ordinarily feel naked without help from both informed discussion and specialized professional studies. Since adversaries will deploy facts and arguments, he had better be prepared.

Even on issues on which partisan politics presses intensely, officials call for analytical inputs. If, for example, wheat prices earned by farmers fall alarmingly, the decline may require verification by statistical techniques, and debate over what to do about it will raise many issues for discussion and perhaps for research. Why the decline? What price levels should be maintained? How does the decline (and attempts at restoration of price) affect the international balance of payments? All such questions call for discussion and research.

Decade by decade, governments enlarge the supply of specialized information and analysis brought to bear on policy making. In the United States, an array of statistical reports—for example, on the number of unemployed, the price level, imports and exports, morbidity and mortality rates, and election returns—steadily expands. Federal government spending on social research has grown prodigiously to a current rate of between $500 million and $1 billion, depending on just what counts as

[2]We want to ask about all kinds of fact gathering, study, discussion, research, and processing of information pertinent to policy making. For emphasis or nuance, in some contexts we shall specify one or another of these terms. Usually "analysis" will stand for all of them.

research.[3] Government calls on universities for help. It also has established or employs the services of many specialized research institutes like the RAND Corporation, originally created by the U.S. Air Force.

From time to time, changes in governmental organization reflect an attempt to concentrate additional analytical fire-power on policy. Thus the federal government established the Budget Bureau in 1921, later reorganized as the Office of Management and Budget in order to take up new analytical tasks. In 1974, the establishment of the Congressional Budget Office brought a new analytic staff to serve Congress.

Formal Planning

Governments also seek analysis of the interrelations among their policies in various areas or over time, a kind of analysis sometimes called planning. A town planning and zoning commission analyzes policies pertaining to land use. The U.S. President's Council of Economic Advisers provides advisory coordination to public policies on employment, the price level, the balance of payments, and economic growth. In Great Britain, the National Economic Development Council, like the French *Commissariat du Plan,* permits the government to achieve a more informed coordination of price, investment, employment, and foreign trade policies.

Nongovernmental Analytical Inputs

In a wealthy country like the United States, analysis pertinent to policy comes to be a massive process engaging millions of citizens and groups. Private corporations, interest groups, universities, and research institutions create a huge flow of unsolicited studies on policy. Through their books and articles, even unaffiliated persons become important to the analysis of policy. Beyond explicit policy analysis runs a deep and wide river of information and opinion fed by many springs, from formal research projects to "letters to the editor," into which policy makers dip for their purposes.[4] The flow of analysis is thinner in poor countries that cannot afford it. In authoritarian countries, governments stifle it.

THE PROFESSIONAL "POLICY ANALYST"

Over the years new techniques arise—cost-benefit studies, operations research, systems analysis, mathematical programming—along with some embellishments that fail, as did the controversial attempt to com-

---

[3]For discussion, see National Research Council, Committee on Social Research and Development, "The Federal Investment in Knowledge of Social Problems" (mimeographed, August 25, 1977), chapter 2.

[4]For a survey, see F. Machlup, *The Production and Distribution of Knowledge in the United States* (Princeton, N.J.: Princeton University Press, 1962).

bine program budgeting with systems analysis known as PPB (Planning-Programming-Budgeting).

One often finds these techniques used in projects going by the name of "policy analysis." Although we use the term "analysis" as a convenient shorthand for all kinds of policy information, discussion, and analysis, "policy analysis" often refers more narrowly to a family of specific forms of professional analysis. In its most fully developed forms, a "policy analysis" formulates the policy problem as a whole, specifying goals and other values, soliciting and evaluating alternative solutions, and identifying the solution that best corresponds to the formulated values.[5] It differs from analysis of a piece of a problem, as when a social scientist studies the high costs of medical care. Although also useful, the latter embraces only a fragment of the considerations pertinent to a policy decision on medical care.

Professional Evaluation

Professional policy evaluation, the professional study of an agency's successes and failures in a policy or program, illustrates the efforts of some to raise the level of rationality in policy making. Ideally, evaluation studies provide feedback; by disclosing what went right or wrong with the last step in policy, they guide the next steps.

Some agencies by law must make explicit evaluations of their own successes and failures; others do so out of prudence. The Department of Health, Education, and Welfare, for example, undertakes evaluation through, among other channels, the office of Assistant Secretary for Planning and Evaluation. Many agencies employ permanent staff or in-house evaluation and also hire outside research or consulting firms to evaluate programs. Government organizations with supervisory functions, among them the General Accounting Office, also make systematic evaluations. The Office of Management and Budget, which after the decline of PPB tried a new method of evaluation called Management by Objective (MBO), continues to search for improved methods of evaluation. Congress itself undertakes evaluation, both through committee hearings and through systematic staff evaluation.

One of the most remarkable attempts at professional evaluation comes from the New Jersey Guaranteed Income Experiments. To determine whether guaranteed incomes would undercut incentives to work, the Office of Economic Opportunity undertook, through the University of Wisconsin's Institute for Research on Poverty, an experiment with

[5]Simply to identify these aspects of "policy analysis" and systems analysis is to put their best foot forward. In the next chapter, we shall see difficulties not apparent here. On how far these methods depart from their idealized form, there is now substantial literature. For example, see Harvey Sapolsky, *The Polaris Missile System Development* (Cambridge, Mass.: Harvard University Press, 1972).

more than a thousand families. Each family received outright cash income from the experimenters, and its effects on incentives to work were then compared with those from a control group without cash payments. With that historic experiment, professional evaluation acquired a new importance in policy making. Other follow-up experiments continued.

In their desire to prove that their programs have succeeded, policy makers often distort evaluation. In the now notorious evaluation of the Head Start program, a program designed to give disadvantaged children a head start in kindergarten or first grade, many administrators of the program first opposed evaluation. When an evaluation, undertaken over their objections, began to reveal adverse findings, the Office of Economic Opportunity, responsible for the program, tried to suppress distribution of the report.

Many institutions, including the University of California's Graduate School of Public Policy and Harvard University's Graduate Program in Public Policy, now offer professional training in evaluation and other kinds of policy analysis. Several university schools of business have also added policy tracks to their programs.

Distinctive Qualities in Professional Analysis

In the growing professionalism of policy evaluation and other policy analysis, advocates of professional analysis often claim that, unlike most deliberations on policy, their work is systematic, therefore often comprehensive rather than fragmentary concerning the issues at hand, and dispassionate rather than partisan.[6] Indeed, it is often systematic. It attempts to map out the various factors pertinent to the issue at hand and to organize the treatment of them in systematic interrelationship with each other: hence its great dependence on mathematical models for achieving a tight, logical interrelationship of parts. Some people dispute the claim that it is comprehensive (for reasons we shall explore in the next chapter). Clearly, however, a systematic search for relevant variables results in some degree of comprehensiveness. Similarly, some critics deny that it can avoid partisanship, since everyone, they argue, favors some causes or values over others.

Partisanship we shall also examine in the next chapter. We take note here, however, of one kind of partisanship in policy analysis usually thought acceptable to professional policy analysis. Professional analysts, by definition, are committed to evidence and disciplined analysis. They become partisans, sometimes passionately so, on behalf of reason, even if they slide into partisanship on behalf of other causes as well.[7]

Specifically, they often are useful in seeking "efficient" solutions to

---

[6]For example, see Charles L. Schultze, *The Politics and Economics of Public Spending* (Washington, D.C.: Brookings Institution, 1968).
    [7]*Ibid,* pp. 95–96.

problems. In this context, "efficient" means a solution that incorporates elements advantageous to all the participants and their constituencies. Left to themselves, the participants themselves do not always discover them. Professional analysts become experts in seeking approximations of what economists call *Pareto*-efficient solutions, solutions which, compared to the existing state of affairs, benefit all or benefit some parties without injuring any others. Their analysis might show, for example, that certain reductions in railroad freight rates could benefit rail users through savings to them and at the same time benefit the railroads by encouraging increased traffic and revenue.

Professional analysts also often speak as partisans for long-term values—for example, concerned about exhaustion of energy resources or kinds of environmental pollution that become a problem only in the distant future, or about deforestation. That partisan bias probably is useful in correcting the shorter-term biases of most other participants in policy making.

DOES ANALYSIS REALLY COUNT?

Habits of thought often lead us to fear that analysis lays no more than a genteel veneer on conflict that participants will actually settle by some test of strength—votes, political bargaining, scheming and maneuvering, or even bullets. Does analysis really count?

Practical policy makers seem to think so. A recent Budget Bureau Director says:

> The cynical view of the matter is that rational calculation in government programming is a harmless but ineffectual pursuit, since all important questions are ultimately decided on 'political' ground. . . . The thesis is wrong if it is taken to mean the findings of skilled and objective analysis of public programs are not influential and, not infrequently, decisive.[8]

Nevertheless, the voice of reason often reaches no audience. In particular, one might add, a great deal of professional analysis by academic and other analysts is wasted. Government officials often say that they do not find what is offered them useful, and professional analysts say that officials ignore their results. The problem has given rise to a spate of studies on obstructions to social research in policy making.[9] We shall look into these obstructions in the next chapter.

---

[8]U.S., Congress, House, Committee on Government Operations, Research and Technical Programs Subcommittee, *The Use of Social Research in Federal Domestic Programs*, Part I, 90th Cong., 1st sess., April 1967, p. 2.

[9]For example, see a collection of studies in Carol H. Weiss, ed., *Using Social Research in Public Policy Making* (Lexington, Mass.: D.C. Heath and Co., 1977). See also Charles E. Lindblom and David K. Cohen, *Usable Knowledge* (New Haven, Conn.: Yale University Press, 1979).

CHAPTER THREE

LIMITS ON ANALYSIS AS AN ALTERNATIVE TO POLITICS

Having surveyed the many uses of analysis in policy making, we now need to examine its limits. Why, given its obvious merits, do governments not make more use of analysis? Why not less politics and more analysis? What stands in the way?

A conventional explanation points to an inadequate supply of fact, debate, and research in policy making. No such problem exists. Available printed material on each of hundreds of policy problems like school reform, busing, or occupational retraining runs to hundreds of thousands of pages, almost all of it in excess of what any chief executive, legislator, or administrator has time to read. A single study of the prospective environmental impact of a new breeder reactor totaled ten volumes and thousands of pages. A presidential advisor says: "Our policy makers do not lack advice; they are in many respects overwhelmed by it."[1] We shall have to look elsewhere for an explanation—into the various qualities, rather than the supply, of analysis.

To bring out the limitations of analysis as an alternative to politics, let us imagine a situation in which policies can be decided upon wholly by analysis—without any politics, without anyone's exercising control or power over anyone else, without any disputes except those which can be settled by information and thoughtful investigation. We then can see how politics creeps in as a response to various shortcomings of analysis.

To begin with, if we imagine a situation without politics, one wholly

[1]Henry A. Kissinger, *The Necessity for Choice* (New York: Harper & Row, Publishers, 1961), p. 351.

dependent on analysis, we must assume that for any given problem all analysts will come to the same conclusion. (If not, only some kind of political action—voting, for example—could resolve their differences.) They could arrive at such an agreement only if none of them made any mistake of fact or logic, for if they made mistakes they would diverge in their policy conclusions. In short, we have to assume infallible analysis if we wish to avoid a political element in policy making.

Moreover, citizens must believe in the infallibility of the analysts. For if they do not, they will reject the analysts' conclusions; and consequently again they will have to use political means to reach a policy decision.

In addition, the analysts must find that policies best for any one group in society are also best for all other groups. Otherwise, the groups not favored by the chosen policy would not find it the right one for them. Analysis would provide them with no ground for accepting the policy. Again, only a political process like voting or authoritative decree could settle the dispute. Analytical solutions to policy questions thus require a harmony of interests or values among individuals and groups in society.

Some people may think they see an escape from the last requirement. Even assuming that there exists no harmony of interests, that when some people gain from a policy others lose, could analysts not find a solution to the question of how to distribute the gains and losses? If they could, then analysts could determine which policy makes the best of a conflict situation. But this escape route ends at a brick wall. Analysts could determine how to distribute gains and losses only if there existed some accepted criteria for doing so. Such criteria they lack, although each may propose his or her own preferred criteria. Again, only a political process could settle their dispute.

Exclusively analytical policy making would also require that analysis be completed in the time and with the resources available.

Finally, analysis could eliminate the need for politics only if, in addition to all the above conditions, the very definition of society's problems could be made analytically. Otherwise, disputes over which problems to attack would call for a political settlement.

In short, analytical policy making is inevitably limited—and must allow room for politics—to the degree that:

1. It is fallible, and people believe it to be so.
2. It cannot wholly resolve conflicts of value and interests.
3. It is too slow and costly.
4. It cannot tell us conclusively which problems to attack.

Let us see now why each requirement is beyond reach.

THE DEFAULT OF ANALYSIS

Fallibility

Obviously, analysis is fallible. No one, for example, knows all the reasons "why Johnny can't read." For all their accomplishments, economists do not now know enough to cope with simultaneous inflation and unemployment. Analysts and policy makers lack sufficient knowledge of problems like drug abuse, criminal rehabilitation, remedy of educational disadvantage, or occupational retraining. People in policy research and analysis themselves quickly acknowledge their fallibility. For example, an economist, now research head of the Congressional Budget Office, offers an opinion which would command broad agreement. "Considerable progress," she writes, "has been made in identifying and measuring social problems in our society." Moreover, "systematic analysis has improved our knowledge of the distribution of the initial costs and benefits of social action programs." Yet it remains true, she adds, that "little progress has been made in comparing the benefits of different social action programs," and "little is known about how to produce more effective health, education, and other social services."[2]

The basic difficulty stems from a discrepancy between the limited cognitive capacities of the human animal and the complexities of policy problems. Even when extended by a range of devices from written language to electronic computers, the mind at its best simply cannot grasp the complexity of reality.

According to one well recognized formulation, the principle of "bounded rationality,"

> The capacity of the human mind for formulating and solving complex problems is very small compared with the size of the problems whose solution is required for objectively rational behavior in the real world—or even for a reasonable approximation to such objective rationality.[3]

Take even an extremely simple policy problem, much less complex than most national problems. Should a city government introduce one-way traffic on a downtown street? Policy makers cannot know the effects on traffic (including diversion of congestion to other streets), on convenience of the citizens, and on the profitability of businesses in the area. Can analysis answer these questions? It can offer only inconclusive estimates. Analysis can indicate only a variety of possibilities and probabilities.

[2]Alice M. Rivlin, *Systematic Thinking for Social Action* (Washington, D.C.: Brookings Institution, 1971), p. 7.
[3]Herbert A. Simon, *Models of Man* (New York: John Wiley and Sons, Inc., 1957), p. 198.

Transitory and Lasting Difficulties.   Among the most conspicuous in-adequacies of analysis, one is that much of it is not very analytical but often is poorly informed, superficial, biased, or mendacious. Professional analysts also often blunder into tasks beyond their skills. Some analysis makes shoddy attempts to prove by specious means what someone has already decided he wants to think. A more benign view of contemporary analysis is that the problem lies not in turpitude but in insufficiently developed scientific and analytical techniques. Yet in either of these inter-pretations, it follows that the difficulties will persist for a long time.

Moreover, the very best analysis never rises to infallibility. At any one time, some of the world's best economists work as members or staff employees of the President's Council of Economic Advisors. Yet other excellent economists routinely challenge their findings, their theory, and their recommendations. Similarly, excellent sociologists and psycholo-gists have undertaken elaborate studies of the effects of school desegre-gation on educational accomplishment of students, only to find their conclusions declared unsatisfactory by no less excellent colleagues.

Too Much and Too Little Information.   An analyst or policy maker who tries to grapple with the complexity of social problems is caught between the devil and the deep. On the one hand, he or she lacks sufficient information, not knowing what the consequences of one-way traffic might be, or "why Johnny can't read," or whether employment will rise or fall in the coming six months. Suppose, then, the analyst seeks further infor-mation. Long before acquiring what is needed, he or she will be overcome with more information than can be digested, managed or processed in the analysis. Many congressional practices can be understood as protections against this kind of information overload. Members of Congress have so little time to think about the hundreds of bills on the agenda that they end up specializing, thus simply following the lead of some other mem-bers on problems outside their specialization.[4] Everyone who wants to think through a policy problem must steer a course between too little and too much information. There exists no path between the two that is not highly fallible.[5]

Difficulties proliferate and likelihood of error becomes all the

[4] For a vivid detailed account of how carefully a U.S. senator must allocate his time to no more than a selected few policy problems in order to avoid overload, see Elizabeth Drew, "Senator," *New Yorker,* September 11 and 18, 1978.

[5] A peculiar and not widely understood phenomenon in professional analysis is that it often does not move toward answers but spawns new questions. The famous Coleman report on the effect of school policies on student learning and achievement is an example. Although excellent scholars spent $2 million on an assiduous study, its effect was to begin a vast new controversy as new contingencies were discovered in the relationship between school and learning. James S. Coleman and others, *Equality and Educational Opportunity* (U.S., Department of Health, Education, and Welfare, 1966).

greater because society, its problems, and people's responses to them constantly change. By the time that a policy maker or analyst learns, for example, that inflation and unemployment do not occur together and comes to understand why not, it turns out that the institutional structure of the economy has subtly changed in such a way that they now appear simultaneously. Just such a change in recent years has upset a great deal of our knowledge of the American economy.

Many leaders and ordinary citizens doubt, in any case, what they hear from social scientists, researchers, and other investigators of social problems and solutions. When economists, for example, began years ago to argue that governments could safely run deficits, that an unbalanced budget in government meant something quite different from an unbalanced budget for an individual or a business enterprise, the challenge of that view to "common sense" went beyond what many people could accept. The most perceptive skeptics, one might add, could see that the new doctrine rested not on scientific fact, but rather on a mixture of reasonably (but not conclusively) grounded empirical knowledge and advice, the latter embodying certain professional norms (or biases) favored by economists.

One often hears the complaint that lawmakers, other policy makers, and citizens resist using the information and analysis available to them because they are ignorant, stubborn, or irrationally hostile to rational problem solving. They often are. Yet when one authority offers a finding or recommendation on policy and another immediately disputes it, people often do not know whom to believe. Much of their resistance to proferred information and analysis reveals nothing more than wise skepticism about all information and analysis when they cannot distinguish the good from the bad.

Conflict of Values

Nor can analysis resolve all conflicts of values and interests. Analysis cannot find policies unequivocally good for all; if good for some groups, they damage others. In that case, we noted that an analytical solution to policy choices requires an overriding criterion through which it can be decided which groups shall benefit and which ones lose.

But over two thousand years of sophisticated philosophical inquiry have so far failed to produce an adequate criterion. How can we know the right distribution of income and wealth? By what final criterion does analysis justify dangerous technology when it benefits some people and hurts others? How much should one generation sacrifice for the benefit of another? You and I each may have confident answers to these questions, but established criteria do not exist. Analysis will not reach a conclusion.[6]

For some conflicts, many of us endorse the criterion that majority preferences should prevail over minority preferences. But no one holds to such a principle for all cases. For example, we do not use it to justify taking the assets of or enslaving a minority for the benefit of a majority.

On close inspection, the majority criterion holds only in special cases: only some tiny fraction of governmental decisions can be put to a vote. Some people in every society flatly deny the virtue of the criterion altogether.

The Public-Interest Criterion.   Does the concept of the public interest provide a criterion for policy analysis?[7] For you to say, "air pollution control serves the public interest," may mean that you believe that pollution harms not just you but many other people as well and that you think the gains from controlling it would be worth their cost. That kind of statement, however, does not mean that anyone agrees with you or that you are right. Sometimes "public interest" refers to some universal good, that is, to certain values believed to serve everyone in the society. We do not know, in fact, which values are of this kind.[8]

---

[6]To be sure, many evaluative statements can be interpreted as empirical propositions and thus can be objectively tested. These are statements intended to be taken as true or false according to some accepted criteria. Take, for instance, the statement, "everyone should have a good job." I may believe that everyone should have a good job because everyone ought to be well fed and housed. If so, the statement can be interpreted to mean that people with good jobs in fact will be well fed and well housed. Whether that is true or false can be tested empirically.

Similarly, under some circumstances one can test the proposition that everyone ought to be well fed and well housed. If it means, "people who are well fed and housed will be happy," it is an empirical proposition in form, in principle empirically verifiable. As we move on through such chains or linkages, however, we will increasingly run into woozy abstractions like "happiness" that make empirical propositions containing them impossible to confirm in practice. In any case, one eventually arrives at the end of the line at which some final evaluative propositions, because they cannot be examined in the light of still some further linked proposition, are impossible to verify empirically even in principle. The dominant view in contemporary social science is that these end-of-the-line propositions are impossible to verify both in principle and practice.

[7]On the concept and the literature on it, see the article "Public Interest," in the *International Encyclopedia of the Social Sciences* (New York, Macmillan Co., 1968).

[8]**Utility theory:** The eighteenth-century utilitarian Jeremy Bentham thought he had found in the principle "the greatest good for the greatest number" a criterion for policy analysis on which agreement should be possible. The egalitarian spirit of his principle was not universally acceptable, and in addition, his principle was logically defective. For the greatest good cannot simultaneously be given to the greatest number; to give more privileges or benefits to A so that A can enjoy the greatest good is to withhold them from B.

Responding to the technical difficulty in the principle, economists have explored the possibility that the maximization of total utility (of satisfaction) in society might be a universally acceptable criterion for policy. The best policy, they proposed, would be one

Time and Cost

Analysis also runs afoul of the requirement that it be completed in the time and with the resources available. Most policy decisions are made using no more than perfunctory analysis, because decisions cannot wait until "all the facts are in." Sustained analysis requires not hours, days, or weeks, but months or years. Social scientists have now been working for at least two decades on analyzing the effects of school desegregation on students' educational accomplishment but have not yet agreed on an answer.

Because analysis takes time, it eats up resources. Because during each day a public official must make many decisions, he or she would exhaust the budget if many of the problems became research projects. Because analysis is in any case fallible, the public official will often wisely refuse to invest heavily in it. No government has yet financed a massive near-conclusive research project on any policy choice, even as an experiment in order to see how much it would cost to do so; costs prohibit it.

In all societies, therefore, most policy questions are decided by faster, cheaper methods than by analysis: for example, by elections, by legislative voting, or, much more often, by delegating responsibility for decisions to some designated official who must decide the question, whether or not there are time and funds for analysis.

Problem Formulation

Finally, a purely analytic, nonpolitical solution to the very question of how the policy problem ought to be formulated is itself impossible. As we have seen, policy makers do not face a given problem. Instead they must identify and formulate their problem. Street violence increases in American cities. What is the "real" problem? Decline of law and order? Racial and ethnic discrimination? Impatience of minorities with the pace of reform? Incipient revolution? Low income? Lawlessness at the fringe of an otherwise relatively peaceful reform movement? Urban disorganization? Alienation?

Although analysis can help in answering all such questions, it cannot answer them fully. At some point, the question of how to formulate the problem calls for an act of choice or will. Of the various ways to formulate and attack the problem or problems just illustrated, there exists no cor-

---

which created the largest amount of "want-satisfaction" in the society. They discovered that their principle was defective on many counts. For example, some people simply do not believe that want-satisfaction is acceptable as a criterion; some wants, they think, ought not to be satisfied. Many people also believe that some people's wants are less important than other people's, hence do not believe in simply maximizing want-satisfaction, but instead wish to achieve some specific distribution of want-satisfaction—a distribution in favor of, for example, Aryans, whites, Hindus, Europeans, the rich, the old families, proletarians, the landed aristocracy, and so forth.

rect and incorrect way between which analysis can choose. Such questions, moreover, contain moral components. They cannot be fully settled except by reference to values or interests in conflict in any society. The settlement requires politics rather than analysis.

CHAPTER FOUR

PARTISAN ANALYSIS

All these shortcomings of analysis in policy making bring us back again to the necessity for politics. In reconsidering the relation between analysis and politics, we shall move to a new view of analysis.

INTERACTIVE POLICY MAKING

Let us go back to the distinction between analysis and politics in policy making. When we say that policies are decided by analysis, we mean that an investigation of the merits of various possible actions has disclosed reasons for choosing one policy over others. When we say that politics rather than analysis determines policy, we mean that policy is set by the various ways in which people exert control, influence, or power over each other.[1] A ruler decrees a policy. Or a legislature votes one. Or the citizens cast ballots that authorize the winner of the election to exercise the policy-making authority of the presidency. Or two political adversaries scheme against each other in any one of many possible ways, ranging from assassination to one's hiring away the other's staff.

Each of these political ways of setting a policy in some degree substitutes action for analysis. Instead of thinking through a problem to find a solution, the solution follows acts like voting, negotiating, or silencing an opponent. In personal decision making, people often also substitute act for analysis, as when they flip a coin to decide what to do.

Because in complex social problem solving people act on each other, action becomes interaction. In interaction people exert control over each other. They often do so without intending to and without

[1]We shall use the single term "control" to represent all three terms.

awareness, as when street demonstrators who intend only to influence legislators inadvertently create a backlash effect among their fellow citizens.

In many areas of life other than government, problem solving through interaction also often takes the place of analysis. In contemporary Western societies, for example, market interactions—buying and selling—"solve" the problem of the uses to which the nation's resources should be allocated. No one needs to analyze that problem. By contrast, in Soviet-style systems, planners try to analyze it.

To identify interaction as an alternative to analysis makes a point not quite so simple as first appears. We do not simply allege that people interact with each other. That hardly needs saying. Nor do we simply point out that interactions often implement policies, as when administrators employ a system of income reporting and enforcement of payment to implement tax laws. Nor, for that matter, do we simply say the opposite, that interactions often interfere with the implementation of some policies, as when people riot or evade the law. Although all true, none of these propositions makes the point intended. Our point is that interactions themselves often solve, resolve, or ameliorate problems. Interactions set or make policy. As problem-solving and policy-making processes, interactions constitute an alternative to analysis.

In governmental policy making, political interactions can always replace analysis and indeed can often reach solutions when analysis cannot. If, for example, each of a large number of disputing people has a stake in how a problem might be solved, it may not be possible, as we have seen, to reach through analysis a reconciliation of their differences. But the particular method of interaction called voting can often make the decision easy. As another example, if a government decides to control wage rates in order to head off inflation, the task of setting the right wage levels may run beyond anyone's analytical capacity (or, for reasons discussed in the preceding chapter, analysis may not be trusted). In that case, a form of interaction called bargaining among representatives of management, workers, and public in a tripartite wage board can set wages.

The most frequent way to solve a governmental policy problem that no one can analyze adequately is through a form of interaction called delegation. Responsibility for making the decision is delegated to some designated official. Such an official may, of course, then try to analyze the problem. But he may not. He instead may toss a coin, decide the issue by some rule of thumb, indulge his own prejudices thoughtlessly, or perhaps delegate the decision again to someone else. Whatever he does, the act of delegation to him produces a decision not dependent on analysis. (And, depending on how he makes the decision—for example, what rule of thumb he uses, if any, or what qualities of judgment or prejudice he brings to the decision—one might think the decision better than would have been achieved through analysis.)

THE CONSEQUENT ALTERED ROLE FOR ANALYSIS

Great implications for analysis in policy making follow from the above. Because interactions set policy, as at least in part they always do, analysis in fact usually plays a role different from what we have seen so far. The kind of analytic policy making so far discussed—analysis as an alternative to politics—does not represent the typical use of analysis in policy making. Not usually an alternative to politics, analysis commonly operates as an indispensable element in politics. It becomes a method of exerting control. Rather than making frontal attacks on policy problems, it more often meets certain needs of people, especially officials, to control others in political interaction. This it does in ways we can specify.

Analysis Made Helpful to Interactive Role

Various participants in political interaction use analysis to improve the way they play their interactive roles. If, as an alternative to researching a question of policy, it is put to a vote, individuals may wish to use analysis in order to decide for whom or for what to vote (just as participants in market buying and selling analyze what to buy or sell). Or negotiators analyze the various stands they might take in bargaining. In any of these cases, any person's analysis operates as an instrument of control over others.

Take note that analytical tasks become easier when analysis plays such a part in interaction. The simplification of analytical task is clearest in market interactions. To analyze a potentially profitable sale or purchase calls for less study than to analyze the whole problem of resource allocation or income distribution for the economy. Similarly, in political interaction, a good environmental policy may require feats of analysis far greater than those required from a negotiator who wants no more than to negotiate efficiently. An individual voter may of course consider the whole nation's problems in deciding how to vote, but most voters analyze their voting options much more simply. The reduction in complexity makes this kind of analysis feasible when analysis as an alternative to politics breaks down in the face of complexity.

How well analysis adapts to interaction varies greatly from one participant to another. In market interaction, the leading participants, business executives, are relatively clearheaded about their roles in the process. They see their task as making money. As a result they often have an appetite for whatever analysis will help them perform that task. They do not want analysis of how the economy ought to be organized or on whether it would be good for society to produce, for example, fewer automobiles and more low-cost housing. They represent an example of participants in interaction who often efficiently adapt their analytical needs to their roles in interaction.

For participants in governmental interaction, roles are less well defined than in the market. Should the Secretary of Energy, for example, pursue his own broad version of the public interest? Or focus on conserving energy, leaving to other officials responsibilities for other dimensions of the public interest? Or implement the President's policies? Or, like a corporate executive, see to it that the department grows? Uncertain about his own role, he remains uncertain about the kinds of analysis that can help most in his role. He may spend heavily on analytical inputs only to find them not usable, a common phenomenon in government.[2]

Analysis as an Instrument of Persuasion

In order to play an interactive role in, for example, policy making on federal aid to public education, a member of congress will assess (either informally or through staff aides) the present state of the schools, current controversies, the direction of movement in policy in recent years, and the array of policies currently under consideration. Members will also ask some questions that reflect their position as officials of the federal government in a policy area in which state and local governments are also active: Can we use federal policy to stimulate the states and localities to do their job better? Can we keep the costs of education from shifting from them to the federal government? In addition, they will ask a number of questions pertinent to their particular positions in political interaction, such as: Considering my constituents, what position should I espouse? Considering congressional leadership and my hope for congressional allies, what position should I take? How much of my energy should I invest in educational policy making, at the cost of attention to other policy areas? Can I get help from any of the education interest groups?

If all these questions are analyzed, the work has only begun. In interaction, the legislator must go on to ask how to influence or control other participants: How can we motivate the states and localities to do their jobs? How can I induce those of my constituents who will not like the policies I espouse to forgive or, more likely, to forget? How can I induce at least a few of my congressional colleagues to join me in sponsoring a bill or in getting a favorable recommendation for my bill from the relevant congressional committee? In short, the legislator understands that analysis is needed not only to clarify his or her own position but to bring other participants around to this position.

[2]Carol H. Weiss, *Using Social Research in Public Policy Making* (Lexington, Mass.: D. C. Heath and Co., 1977).

Among the possibilities open for bringing others around to this position, persuasion stands out as one of the most important, perhaps the most powerful method. To be persuasive, however, especially with other knowledgeable officials and activists in policy making, calls for analysis to do yet another task. The legislator must analyze how they see their interests, what they want in policy. He or she must also analyze why his or her preferred policies will suit their interests, that is, will give them what they want. (He may, in doing so, find it advantageous to shift his policy preferences so as to make them more attractive to those participants he wants to influence or control.) Analysis as an instrument of persuasion thus emerges as a distinctive major use of analysis in political interaction.

Persuasion stands as a fundamental feature of all political systems. Feared as a source of control, most governments try to curb it, and only democratic governments allow analysis and persuasion relatively free play. Evidence of the power of persuasion lies everywhere: in the degree to which authoritarian rulers, who have many other powers at their disposal, rely on it in the form of propaganda and other forms of indoctrination; in the budgets that corporations allocate to advertising; and in the sums spent on political campaign and interest-group public relations in the democracies.

Much persuasion works by simple repetition of message or by pageantry or other display that sweeps away one's critical judgment. But, on the other hand, much of it rests on analysis. Especially among political leaders, including civil servants, persuasion relies on the communication of critical facts and analyses. A senator, for example, persuades a colleague to support a bill by showing the colleague its analyzed consequences for national defense or for some other concern. A senator gains a reputation as especially influential because he or she "has the facts." The persuasive power of information and analysis also stimulates the common complaint among legislators that they come to be the prisoners of civil servants, or sometimes of lobbyists, who have the relevant facts at their command. Anyone who claims to know—and goes unchallenged —that this cannot be done or that is the one and only alternative open, can achieve great effect on a decision.

The great influence of persuasive analysis leads some observers to suggest that analysts, intellectuals, or persons with a special analytical capacity constitute a rising elite in contemporary political systems. Such an elite comes to be more conspicuous as the prestige of analysis intensifies with the technical complexity of policy making in the modern world. In a field like international relations, for example, the many informal conferences arranged by the Council on Foreign Relations and its journal, *Foreign Affairs,* constitute forums in which the knowledgeable discuss policy with great effect on the governmental policy makers who are among them. Such an elite of knowledgeables is the first of several that we shall meet in our exploration of policy making.[3]

Two Routes to Persuasion Through Analysis.   Persuasive analysis usually works to the degree that people are genuinely persuaded by it. Yet it achieves an effect in some circumstances without actually persuading. To grasp this unfamiliar second possibility, one has to understand that in many circumstances persons in conflict do not want a dispute to escalate. They will often agree to terminate a dispute by following some rule—for example, a rule that a vote should be taken. An alternative rule is that the best analysis wins. Administrative policy makers, for example, sometimes follow the tacitly accepted rule that certain kinds of issues are to be considered settled by a competition of analysis. In effect everyone agrees not to go further than that, that is, not to fight harder than with fact and analysis, because escalation beyond that point would demand too much time and energy and would incur too many more risks. The result is that by rule all accept certain solutions, not because actually persuaded of their merits but simply because they have agreed that the decision goes to those who have, by conventional standards, made the best case.

PARTISAN ANALYSIS

To all these uses of analysis as an instrument of control in political interaction, we can give the name partisan analysis. All participants in political interaction in some degree play partisans roles. Each participant presses a point of view, a set of interests. In this sense, an individual voter counts as a partisan. So does a legislator, a civil servant and, of course, an interest-group leader. To label them partisans does not mean that they are all equally narrow in their opinions or equally preoccupied with their own as opposed to broader interests. The legislator, for example, often takes an extremely broad view of national needs and may sometimes step almost wholly out of a partisan role.

Even the President is a partisan. Suppose, for what he considers good reason, he urges a policy on Congress which both House and Senate reject. He sees that, because conflicts of interest are too great, the policy problem is not going to be given an analytical solution but will be decided by political interaction. The President may therefore want to analyze those alternative policies falling within the range of policies acceptable to Congress, however undesirable he thinks they are. Or he may

---

[3]See Seymour Martin Lipset and Asoke Basu, "The Role of the Intellectual and Political Roles," in *The Intelligentsia and the Intellectuals,* ed. Aleksander Gella (Beverly Hills, Ca.: Sage Publications, 1976).

want to look for a new policy possibility that will not suffer from the objections, invalid though he thinks they are, to his unsuccessful policy. Or he may want to analyze possibilities for inducing the House and Senate to reconsider, say by offering congressional leaders a trade for something they want. In short, he will use information, discussion, and research specifically to develop his next moves in winning his conflict with Congress.

Although partisans will use analytical resources only in furthering their own interests, they interact with many other partisans who do the same on behalf of their respective interests. As each feeds analysis into interactive processes for his or her own benefit, at least some of it becomes the common possession of all the participants. Each can then challenge it or use it. If it is helpful to a settlement, it may be seized by all. If it is obstructive, it may be countered by competing analysis. Quite possibly, the fabled "competition of ideas," thought to be essential to pluralist democracy, largely takes the form of exchange among partisan analysts and partisan policy makers who use their analyses. This may be true even if some kinds and degrees of partisanship turn participants toward flagrant misrepresentation and outright falsification.

Extraordinary attempts at and sometimes success in persuasion through partisan analysis have marked some of the high points in American history on occasions in which a political leader sets out to convince the various major groups in the population that each of their interests will be served by their joining a new coalition of interests. Lincoln seems to have seen that to be his task when he tried to transform the debate on slavery into the issue of the survival of the Union. After the Civil War Mark Hanna created around the Republican Party a new configuration of business, labor, and farmer interests in industrialization that became the dominant opinion for decades thereafter and accounted for the long period of predominantly Republican rule in the United States. Franklin Roosevelt also restructured political aspiration and controversy with the New Deal. Leaders who can analyze discord, find some common interests, and persuade each discordant group that its interest lies in pursuing a new set of goals will often take their places in history as the great political figures of their times.[4]

---

[4]See Eric Nordlinger, *Conflict Regulation in Divided Societies* (Cambridge, Mass.: Harvard University Center for International Affairs, 1972).

CHAPTER FIVE

MAKING THE MOST OF ANALYSIS

Many elementary cultural accomplishments extend our problem-solving capacities. Speech itself does so. Written language also does, with all that it implies for so precious a gain as recording information so that we need not solve the same problems over and over again. Quantification does so, because of the skill in measurement that numbers make possible. Even the simple analytic device of "factoring out," dividing a problem into parts, does so.[1]

Other powerful extenders of our analytical capacities include specific processes for rigorous formal analysis: mathematics and logic; the expanding collection of techniques termed "scientific method"; probability theory, through which we extend our capacity to cope with uncertainty; the powerful tool of double-entry bookkeeping, developed in about the thirteenth century; and electronic computation, an accomplishment of the twentieth century.

From unexpected sources comes help in stretching our analytic capacities. For example, a crisis often transforms a policy maker's perceptions (and sometimes also galvanizes energies), with the result that he gets a new grasp on his problem.[2] Although we usually think of a crisis as something to be avoided, certain mild crises, like annual budgeting, can be produced deliberately in order to stimulate the policy maker.

[1]An unusally perceptive and stimulating analysis of precisely how "factoring out" or subdividing problems aids rationality is in H. A. Simon, "The Architecture of Complexity," *Proceedings of the American Philosophical Society,* 106 (December 1962).
[2]For the strengths and weaknesses of crisis decision making, see Irving L. Janis and Leon Mann, *Decision Making* (New York: Free Press, 1977), chapter 3. See also, on the possibility that crisis improves the decision capacity of organizations, H. L. Wilensky, *Organizational Intelligence* (New York: Basic Books, 1967), pp. 76–77.

These methods of extending analytical capacity are as valuable as they are because our minds are as little as they are. Our cognitive limitations compel us to invest heavily in techniques for extending the competence of our minds. Despite these gains, at any given time our cognitive capacity always remains limited, still not up to the complexity of the problems we face in policy making.

Through much of intellectual history and now conspicuously in the literature of public policy making, run two versions—more precisely, visions or ideals—of how a society like ours can further extend the use of the human brain to solve social problems.[3] One emphasizes analysis as an alternative to politics; and the other, analysis as part of political interaction. One therefore emphasizes the conventional view of analysis with which we began; and the other, partisan analysis. In both theory and practice, proponents of each of the two kinds of analysis dispute with each other on how to improve policy making. Although all societies rely on both kinds of analysis, proponents of each push for a larger place for the kind they favor.

SCIENTIFIC AND STRATEGIC POLICY MAKING

One group of proponents believes that the human brain, despite its limitations, can cope well enough, not today or tomorrow but someday, with the complexities of the social world. They therefore want to raise the analytic and lower the political component in policy making. In this vision or ideal, the basic steps in policy making correspond closely to the steps in any scientific effort: one identifies and carefully formulates a problem, canvasses possible solutions, examines painstakingly the suitability of the alternative solutions, and proceeds to a final choice. Proponents of this ideal see good policy making as basically an intellectual rather than political process. If one pushes the ideal to its logical conclusion, which many of its proponents consider too extreme a form, the ideal ruler resembles Plato's philosopher-king and not a person chosen in a political process like voting.

The Strategic Ideal

Proponents of the competing vision or ideal begin with the limited cognitive capacity of the human being. From their sense of its limits, they draw two great strategic inferences. The first calls for the subordination of analysis to interaction, which they see as a fact of life that has to be accepted and hence incorporated into ideals or models of policy making. The second calls for the simplification of analysis in all possible ways, for

[3]For further analysis, see Charles E. Lindblom, *Politics and Markets* (New York: Basic Books, 1977), chapters 19 and 23.

example, by proceeding step by step through trial and error rather than by trying to comprehend a problem in its entirety.

Moreover, because proponents of the strategic ideal see problems as too complex for the human brain, their trust in any one analyst or policy maker does not go very far. Policy-making responsibility should be shared by a plurality of interacting policy makers and analysts. Good policy making requires further that each participant face a variety of challenges, indeed that every alleged fact be subjected to challenges. This is not simply the polite challenge by one analyst or scholar to another (as in the scientific method prized in the first vision above), but it is widespread challenge throughout the society through a plurality of participants in policy making. Because opportunities for challenge will vanish unless carefully protected, the civil liberties become essential to the strategic vision of analytical policy making. Society must seek good policies, or establish facts and find "truth" through the "competition of ideas," not through the analytical skills of a philosopher-king or any comparable elite of intellectuals.

Proponents of the strategic ideal of course endorse the partisan use of analysis. Indeed, they assume that the competition of ideas occurs as a contest among partisans. Only partisans can be counted on, because of their own self-interests, to bring to bear every fact or argument germane to their interests. Their motivation largely powers the never-ending search for "truth" insofar as truth can ever be approximated.

Proponents of the strategic ideal find their vision of policy making confirmed by their belief that, when people differ over values, beyond some point further analysis cannot help and must be supplemented by interactive policy making.

Objections to the Scientific Vision

Proponents of the strategic ideal do not deny the value of bringing science and social science more and more into the service of policy making. But they see the scientific vision or ideal as not very useful because it fails to give guidance. They believe that when scientific problem solvers face a complex problem which they cannot actually master, they fall back on hasty improvisations. By a useful ideal, the strategic advocates mean one like their own, which specifies guidelines such as: accepting the subordination of analysis to politics, creating a competition among analysts, accepting partisanship, and using a variety of simplifications such as trial and error.

Objections to the Strategic Ideal

The proponents of the scientific vision find a great deal wrong with the vision of strategic policy making. They believe that one can test the rationality of a policy only through a more or less scientific analysis of it.

They believe that the crudities of political controversy and of political interaction, in which people coerce and otherwise manipulate each other, cannot substitute for the processes of rational choice. Moreover, partisanship may run into danger. It obscures everyone's understanding rather than achieving a mutual clarification. As for simplifying of problems through such devices as trial and error, they reply sharply: indeed we must employ such simplifications until we know better. But as simplifications rather than fully scientific approaches to problems, they are error prone, hence not worthy of incorporation into ideals or guidelines.

To this last charge, the strategic advocates reply that indeed their simplifications admit error. They even grant that the competition of ideas does so. All problem solving, they believe, does so—dangerously so. The very attempt to extend analysis beyond what it can do and the refusal to develop guidelines for coping with its incapacities—these features of scientific policy making render it also error prone.

Continuing Conflict

We can identify the two groups of proponents. Those of the scientific vision include Plato, Rousseau, Marx (and much of communist theoretical thought), and in the contemporary Western world, some advocates of planning and other kinds of formal problem solving like systems analysis. The principal advocates of the strategic vision include liberal and democratic theorists, especially John Stuart Mill and the English nineteenth century liberals and pluralists, along with a disparate collection of contemporary intellectuals in the natural and social sciences, philosophy, and public affairs who make a case for diversity, conflict, openness, and improvisation as society's main assets in problem solving. Others take the same track because driven into it by their fear of overorganization of society and of a bureaucratic mentality in problem solving at the hands of scientific policy makers.[4]

[4]Among many in this style of thought: for philosophy, Karl Popper, *The Open Society and Its Enemies* (London: G. Routledge and Sons, Ltd., 1945) and Michael Polanyi, *Personal Knowledge* (Chicago: University of Chicago Press, 1958); on science: Thomas Kuhn, *The Structure of Scientific Revolutions* (Chicago: University of Chicago Press, 1962) and Imre Lakatos, "Falsification and the Methodology of Scientific Research Programmes," in *Criticism and Growth of Knowledge*, ed. Imre Lakatos and Allan Musgrave (Cambridge: Cambridge University Press, 1970); for social science: George Simmel, "Conflict" (1908), translated in George Simmel, *Conflict and the Web of Group-Affiliations* (Glencoe, Ill.: Free Press, 1950); Lewis Coser, *The Functions of Social Conflict* (Glencoe, Ill.: Free Press, 1956); Albert O. Hirschman, *The Strategy of Economic Development* (New Haven, Conn.: Yale University Press, 1958); Harvey Liebenstein, "Allocative Efficiency vs. X-Efficiency," *American Economic Review*, 56 (June 1966); Burton Klein, *Dynamic Economics* (Cambridge, Mass.: Harvard University Press, 1977); Richard R. Nelson, "The Economic Problem and the Role of Competition" (Paper presented to the Society of Government Economists, Atlantic City, N.J., September 17, 1976); and Charles E. Lindblom, *The Intelligence of Democracy* (New York: Free Press, 1965).

Some approaches to policy making explicitly combine elements of both visions, and most people carry elements of both in their minds.[5] But the two remain powerful conflicting intellectual currents. From time to time one or the other is refreshed either by new theory or by new practical accomplishments in policy making, such as many of the new techniques of "scientific" policy analysis identified in chapter 2.

Clearly the conflict between the two visions bears not simply on analytical techniques but on the relation of analysis to politics. It raises basic questions about which political structures take most advantage of useful analysis. Pressing as they do toward ever more formal scientific techniques, the advocates of the scientific vision also press toward the kinds of political and administrative organization supporting those techniques. They tend toward centralized authority within the executive and toward moving authority from voters and legislatures into a highly trained bureaucracy.

In contrast, the advocates of the strategic vision are pluralists. They wish to keep authority diffused—in Congress, for example, to many congressional committees. They also tend to find substantial merits in interest-group activity, as well as in broad public debate and group discussion, even if it is not informed by special professional analytical techniques. The two groups also differ in their conceptions of formal planning. The first sees it ideally as analogous to scientific inquiry. The second sees it as the practice of the usual partisan analytical strategies strengthened by special attention to long-range considerations and to broadened interconnections among specific policies.[6]

AGREEMENT IN COMMON PRACTICE

Despite their conflicts, proponents of both ideals agree that in actual practice policy makers and analysts must use various simplifying strategies. For example, an exhaustive search for the maximum, for the best of all possible policies, usually costs more than it is worth. An actual strategy, therefore, instead seeks a level of accomplishment below maximization. If a government finds a satisfactory way to reduce its balance-of-payments deficit, it will not ordinarily look further for a better one. Proponents of both scientific and strategic visions "satisfice" in actual practice, even if the former regards doing so as a regrettable makeshift.[7]

[5]See Amitai Etzioni, "Mixed Scanning: A Third Approach to Decision Making," *Public Administration Review,* 27 (December 1967).

[6]An analysis of planning as in this second school of thought is Dennis A. Rondinelli, "Public Planning and Political Strategy," *Long Range Planning,* 9 (April 1976).

[7]The word and the concept are from H. A. Simon, "A Behavioral Model of Rational Choice," *Quarterly Journal of Economics,* 69 (February 1955).

Seriality

As another example, many policy makers will come to see policy making as a never-ending process in which continual nibbling substitutes for the good bite that may never be offered. In the United States, policy makers nibble endlessly at taxation, social security, national defense, conservation, foreign aid, and the like. They assume that these problems never vanish and hold themselves in readiness to return again and again. The difference between scientific and strategic problem solvers is less in their actual practice than in their attitude toward nibbling.

Strategic problem solvers see nibbling as a strategy for moving through a series of incremental changes in policy. They claim that doing so focuses the policy maker's analysis on familiar, better known experience; sharply reduces the number of alternative policies to be explored; reduces the number and complexity of factors to be analyzed; takes advantage of feedback information;[8] and limits analysis to what is politically feasible.[9] Scientific problem solvers see the same process as indecisive, makeshift, timid, narrow, inconclusive, and procrastinating.

Ideology

As a final example of agreed practice, we find both groups dependent on ideology in analysis. Ideology serves as a conspicuous specialized aid to analysis. A troublesome word, "ideology" has come to mean many things. It may denote any interlocked set of important generalizations about social organization. An example is the American ideology that ties together ideas about democracy, liberty, pluralism, private enterprise, individualism, and social responsibility in a way that guides each American's thinking about public policy. Or it may denote a more formal and highly organized set of such beliefs, like Marxist-Leninist principles.

Any even loosely organized set of interlocking generalizations about social organization greatly helps analysis and is probably indispensable. It appears that all policy analysis depends to a degree on ideology so defined. Even if not dogmatic, a working commitment to

---

[8]Feedback as an aid to decision making has been given its most precise formulation by those who have tried to describe social processes generally as communications processes, taking their lead from N. Wiener, *The Human Use of Human Beings* (Boston: Houghton Mifflin Co., 1950). See also John D. Steinbruner, *The Cybernetic Theory of Decision* (Princeton, N.J.: Princeton University Press, 1974).

[9]Incrementalism as a strategy is discussed at length in David Braybrooke and Charles E. Lindblom, *A Strategy of Decision* (New York: Free Press, 1963). For an example of application to a specific policy area, see A. Wildavsky, *The Politics of the Budgetary Process*, 2nd ed. (Boston: Little, Brown & Co., 1974). For a discussion of the usefulness of such a strategy in a variety of arenas of decision making, see Albert O. Hirschman and Charles E. Lindblom, "Economic Development, Research and Development, Policy Making: Some Converging Views," *Behavioral Science*, 7 (April 1962). For controversy about the strategy, see "Governmental Decision Making," a symposium, *Public Administration Review*, 24 (September 1964), pp. 153–165.

pluralist democracy and corporate enterprise, for example, permits a policy analyst to restrict the search for policies and to simplify the analysis.

In effect, an ideology takes certain beliefs out of the gunfire of criticism, or at least throws up some defense of them. These beliefs, verification of which would require impossible feats of fact-gathering and analysis, therefore can be introduced into analysis as though settled facts.

Even mistaken or overly simple beliefs organize and simplify analysis. If far enough from fact, though, ideology may lead to policies that do not work. Ideology offers a trade-off between simplifying ideas that help and simplifications that hurt.

$$*\quad*\quad*\quad*\quad*\quad*$$

These various strategies for simplification are the last piece of the answer to the question with which we began this series of four chapters: How far do and can information, reasoned discussion, and analysis go in policy making? In these chapters, we have seen what analysis can and cannot accomplish. We have given attention to each of two different kinds of analysis: one as an alternative to politics, the other as part of politics. For improving analytical policy making in the long, long run, we have seen that two schools of thought differ on which of the two kinds to pursue.

Theodore Lownik Library
Illinois Benedictine College
Lisle, Illinois 60532

PART TWO

THE PLAY
OF POWER

CHAPTER SIX

THE PLAY
IN
GENERAL OUTLINE

Because in the real world, analysis is not conclusive, in order to set policy people interact to exercise influence, control, or power over each other. Analysis itself becomes, as we have seen, a method of exerting control. We must now investigate the various interactive control processes, going beyond what we saw of them in the preceding chapters. The political interactions through which people control each other we shall often refer to as the "play of power." Why the term "play"? Because we want to evoke the same meaning as when one speaks of the state of play, say, in a chess or football game or in a complex maneuvering in Congress to override a veto. The "play of power" suggests more complex and closer interconnections than are captured by the flat term "interactions" or by the general term "politics."

Most people know a great deal about the play of power: about who holds formal authority and about ingenious legal and illegal maneuvering among policy-making officials of various kinds and among parties and interest groups. They know also that some participants exercise powers nowhere specified in the written rules of government; that money talks; that politicians sometimes get things done by doing favors for each other and sometimes by killing each other; and that the whole labyrinthian, half-hidden world of politics often makes it impossible to assign responsibility either for achievement or for fiasco in policy making.

First we must identify certain core elements in the play of power in policy making common to all systems, some familiar, some not.

POLICY MAKERS AND ORDINARY CITIZENS

In all national political systems, the active immediate or proximate policy makers are only a tiny proportion of the adult population. Given their control over policy making, they constitute an elite, one composed of chief executives, cabinet members, members of parliament or legislature, policy-making members of the bureaucracy, upper levels of the judiciary, and in some systems, higher levels in the military. The policy-making elite also includes those political bosses and party officals who share actual decision responsibility with government officials. For convenience, we shall call this elite the policy makers.

In all systems, however, even nondemocratic ones, millions of people participate in some way in the play of power in policy making. The largest group of participants, of course, is ordinary citizens, each of whom alone is weak to the point of insignificance. Voting aside, in democratic and many authoritarian systems, ordinary citizens impose constraints on policy makers. If the citizens are treated too badly, their efficiency on the job suffers. Because they need food, training, incentives, policy making must attend to them. Concerned for its citizens, the Soviet Union gives university and postgraduate training to a greater proportion of its citizens than does Great Britain. Decades ago it may have pushed ahead of the United States in subsidized and free medical care.

Some groups of ordinary citizens turn into saboteurs and rebels, as in the repeated, daring uprisings under Poland's authoritarian regime. Yet to play only a minimum role, never insignificant in the play of power, citizens often need neither to speak nor act, if rulers fear that at any time they may do so. They need not deliberately try to achieve control or even realize that they exercise control.

Between policy makers and ordinary citizens, many other specialized participants in policy making play roles differing from system to system: These include interest-group leaders, party workers, journalists and other opinion leaders, businessmen, terrorists, and officials of towns or other subordinate units of government. Another often forgotten group is officials of foreign governments, who can bring influence to bear. Some of the most influential among active participants—interest-group leaders, for example—sometimes move over into the category of policy makers. If, for example, a public official empowered to act on tariff policy dares not do so without consulting with certain major business or union leaders and winning their agreement, they have become policy makers on that issue.

THE PLAY OF POWER ACCORDING TO RULES

With the possible exception of people who are demoralized, everyone lives under a heavy weight of rules constraining behavior. Legal rules, some strong and others weak because not easily enforced, impose some choices on each of us and influence other choices that we remain legally free to make. Zoning laws specify that certain kinds of buildings cannot be built on certain lots. Although within the permitted category of acceptable buildings, the citizen can choose freely, other legal rules—for example, those that regulate parking—will influence the choice.

Moral rules work the same way. So do various self-imposed prudential rules. Some people follow a principle of not drinking coffee after 9:00 P.M., of answering the telephone promptly, or of saving some fixed fraction of each week's income. Like other rules, they vary in effect, some slavishly followed, others, like prohibitions against overeating, often violated, yet invoked occasionally to curb impulsive behavior.

On some spheres of life rules weigh less or more heavily than on others. On consumer behavior they weigh lightly. Consumers cannot legally hire a "hit" man, buy babies, and in some jurisdictions go shopping on Sunday. Beyond these restrictions, customary and prudential rules only loosely regulate their behavior.

Political interaction, the "play of power," is heavily regulated by rules, more so than life in the market place is. A political system is at the core a system of rules specifying the different roles to be played—those of chief executive, legislator, or ordinary citizen, for example. They specify who is eligible to play each role and how persons are to be chosen for them. They also specify what each role player is to be allowed to do or prohibited from doing in the role.

In its heavy dependence on rules, the play of power resembles a game. Political interaction almost never degenerates into a fist fight, and even when it does the combatants usually follow long-established informal rules that prohibit gouging and kicking. Even in armed conflict when the game degenerates, military commanders operate by rules that authorize them to command when they give orders; and their troops follow the rule that they must respond.

The rules laid down in a nation's written constitution, if it has one, may not be among those by which government actually operates. They may be for display, as in the Soviet Union, or transformed through practice and judicial review, as in the United States. Even if effective, the constitutional rules make up only a small number of the hundreds of thousands through which a government operates. Many political rules have no legal status at all. Some are moral (tell the truth), others are expedient (a legislator should not offend the elders in the legislature).

Some people believe that rules do not matter. Some groups, they believe, will inevitably exercise the most control, the rich more than the poor or whites more than blacks. These groups indeed often do exercise disproportionate influence or power. But why? Wealth rests on rules: specifically, the rules of private property. Rules also permit persons to use wealth in many ways that increase their political influence. They permit using funds to obligate candidates to return favors in exchange for campaign contributions. They permit the wealthy to own newspapers or broadcasting facilities.

As for whites, rules again confer advantages on them in the play of power. Rules on property rights long ago held blacks in slavery, and after emancipation, property rules left them impoverished. Rules also prohibited training blacks. In more recent times, rules have often restricted their opportunities. Until recently, for example, admission to leading American private universities was almost entirely closed to blacks. Admissions rules were inconspicuous, because indirect in effect. Rather than specifically identifying blacks as inadmissible, the rules simply identified successful applicants by family background, income, and character of secondary school. Along with other social and legal rules, they effectively cripple blacks in a play of power in which leadership positions go to the educated.

Why People Obey Rules

Participants in the play of power follow rules for diverse reasons. The most common explanation in political science says that participants follow rules because they regard them as legitimate. Alternatively, we often say that people are "forced" to obey rules. "Force" may mean a threat of violence. Or it may refer to some penalty so severe that it leaves no choice. Sometimes the prospective loss of one's friends threatens a severe enough penalty to "force" one to follow rules. As another alternative, people sometimes establish and thereafter obey rules because they see the practical advantage of doing so, as in the signing of the Mayflower Compact by a group of persons who knew they needed a set of rules for their new community. Often no one can say why people obey rules. For example, almost all officials defeated for re-election in the United States follow the rule that they must leave office. Obedience to the rule may be voluntary. Perhaps, however, officials follow it for fear of losing their reputation if they challenge it, for fear of desertion by their staffs, or for fear that others who hold to it can command the military or the police to oust them. The officials may not even pause to ask whether and how they can be made to leave office; they simply assume that they must.

Some Implications

The dependence of the play of power on rules explains the fragility of the political system shown by the frequent ease with which the rules can be set aside rather than obeyed. Nixon gathered around himself a group of associates who tacitly agreed to break many of the rules ordinarily governing the President and his staff. By their own choice, they for some years altered the American political system. In some political systems, a whole corps of top administrators and military leaders will sometimes suddenly, in tacit or explicit agreement, reject the set of rules regulating the play of power. In that way, a coup d'etat abruptly brings down one regime and, with the establishment of a new set of rules, begins another.

Even in time of crisis when, one set of rules having broken down we might imagine force replacing rules, the play of power depends heavily on remaining or new rules. After years of neglecting its responsibilities, when a timid Congress finally began the process of removing Nixon from office, it did so by beginning an elaborate, rule-regulated impeachment process. Anticipating such an outcome, we might imagine Nixon's simply refusing, as some defeated governors have, to leave the executive mansion and trying to carry out his accustomed duties. Or we might imagine, as would happen in some countries, his calling on the military to forbid Congress to convene. Whether Nixon could have succeeded in such efforts would not have depended on his being stronger or more heavily armed than his adversaries. The issue would have been decided against him if the courts and the military had followed the traditional rules. It became clear that almost all the key participants chose or were "forced" to follow the traditional rules regulating impeachment and removal. And Nixon himself finally chose or was "forced" to abide by them.

Even when a revolution sweeps away many old rules governing the play of power, we would find that the revolutionists succeeded only because organized by their own rules. Their seizing power takes the form of their inaugurating a new set of rules governing the new play of power. Even a guerrilla leader can organize a group only if it follows rules.

HOW CONTROL IS EXERCISED IN THE PLAY OF POWER

When participants exert control, influence, or power over each other in a rule-governed or gamelike play of power, just what do they do to each other? One way to exert control is to jail or intimidate one's adversaries. One also can employ softer methods: for example, lie about one's intentions and thus attract allies or silence criticism, or do a favor for a favor. Sometimes one can win on a policy simply by acting in some pivotal way sooner than anyone else does.

It helps to clarify methods of control by noting that many methods operate through rewards and penalties—more precisely through offers of rewards and threats of penalty. People also control each other simply by altering other people's perceptions of probable rewards and punishments, without actually manipulating the rewards and penalties themselves. If you convince me of the advantages to me of what you want me to do and the disadvantages of doing what you do not want me to do, I will do as you say. You may do so by analyzing my situation so that I now see gains or losses I had overlooked. Or you may do so by deceiving me, by leading me to expect nonexistent rewards or penalties, perhaps those that you claim you can bring about even though you cannot. Medicine men, religious leaders, and demagogues often play on gullibility in this way; and so also, sometimes, do presidents and other policy makers.

Persuasion and Partisan Analysis

Both deceitful persuasion and persuasion based on honest analysis of prospective gains and losses are major methods of control in the play of power in policy making. The partisan analysis of the preceding chapter, in which one participant in political interaction tries to show another why the desires of the former will actually benefit the latter, is fundamental to the play of power. A presidential advisor writes: "The essence of a President's persuasive task with Congressmen and everybody else, is to induce them to believe that what he wants of them is what their own appraisal of their own responsibilities requires them to do in their interest, not his."[1] On persuasion and analysis the preceding chapter has already said most of what needs to be said to place them on the list of principal methods of control in the play of power.

Threats

In permitting people to manipulate each other's rewards and penalties, rather than inducing each other to re-evaluate existing gains and losses, societies draw a great distinction between rewards and penalties. Although many societies permit people to try to reward each other, no society permits people freely to threaten or injure each other. The operating rules of most societies permit only certain government officials to threaten or inflict the most severe penalties like incarceration and death, and many societies permit them to do so only in carefully circumscribed conditions. Terrorists understand the power of threats for achieving control and willingly risk breaking rules in order to gain it.

In constitutional democracies, policy makers are constrained, legally and morally, in the injuries they can inflict on each other in political interaction. Perhaps their main threat of injury to other policy makers is to obstruct the other policy maker's program. Depending on the political system and the circumstances, policy makers will also seek to control each other by threats of injuries as varied as loss of job, ruined reputation, alienation of friends and supporters, loss of money, and sometimes assassination.

Exchange

"Exchange" ordinarily refers not to exchange of threats—indeed the use of threat is usually one-sided rather than an exchange—but to an exchange of benefits. I propose that you do something that I want, in which

[1]Richard E. Neustadt, *Presidential Power* (New York: John Wiley and Sons, Inc. 1960), p. 46.

case I will do something that you want. Societies broadly permit people
to control each other in this way since both parties gain. For that reason,
exchange becomes a ubiquitous control in the play of power. It takes
several forms:

Explicit favors. "You go with me this time, and I'll support you
when you need it." Policy makers constantly exchange benefits of this
kind. An exchange of this kind requires a strict *quid pro quo:* each party
specifies just what it wants the other to do.

Reciprocity. A looser form of exchange creates and discharges in-
definite obligations of reciprocity. A legislator does another a favor, as
a result of which sooner or later he or she can make some claim on the
other. The influence of many political officials derives in part from their
success, through favors done for others, in accumulating vast stocks of
political obligations, like money in the bank, which can be cashed as
needed.

Money. The most common form of control through exchange is
buying the responses one wants. In politics, one buys rather than commands the services of a campaign staff, journalists, and broadcasters. One
often can also buy legal and illegal political favors, such as tax favors,
exemption from regulations, or desired legislation. High priced benefits
like these go to people who can spend heavily. Others gain a little control
through offering their meager funds to support organizations such as the
National Urban League or Common Cause to support their political
activity. Why does money play so critical a part in exchange in the play
of power—why not simply an exchange of other benefits? Obviously
benefits in the form of money can reach far and wide, precisely measured
out to achieve just the response desired. And money is a benefit with
universal appeal.

If correct, that argument would imply that those who have a great
deal of money might overwhelm all others in the play of power, going so
far as to pay officials for whatever benefits they might desire. Recognizing
just that possibility, societies by rule restrict the use of money. In most
governments, the rules try to prohibit any person from paying another
person to make political decisions one way rather than another. Rules
forbid buying a vote, a favorable decision from a judge, or a legislator's
or administrator's decision. The result is that in all systems, the United
States, the United Kingdom, and the Soviet Union alike, the rules drive
the buying of political favors underground. In its subterranean circula-
tion, no one can gauge the influence of money on policy making. That
people in politics understand that their money gives them great advantage is indicated by their frequent willingness to break the law in order
to route it to public officials, as well as their willingness to run the risks

of expensive and fallible systems of "laundering" their contributions through intermediaries.

AUTHORITY

Although persuasion and exchange might rank as the most frequently employed methods of control in the play of power, another method—authority—is no less important and on several counts occupies a more basic or fundamental place in the play of power. Indeed, the proposition that government is at root an authority system would command wide support among political scientists.

What we here call authority can best be understood if we distinguish two routes by which people use various methods of control. In one the controllers use various methods of control (persuasion, threat, or offer of benefit, among others) on the persons they wish to control on each and every occasion when they want to control them. In the other, they use these same methods only occasionally in order to induce the persons they wish to control to accept a standing rule of obedience to them.[2] The second, and only the second, establishes authority: If I follow a rule of obedience to you, you have authority over me.

Employers and supervisors in business enterprises, for example, do not usually manipulate, persuade, or otherwise induce their employees to do what management wants them to do each time they want a response. Instead, the employer pays the employees to accept a rule of obedience: to do by rule whatever employer or supervisor asks them to do. The employees are paid to accept managerial authority on the job. Soldiers in the field do not usually do as their officers command because of ad hoc manipulation, threat or offer of benefit, for example, to enforce each command on each occasion. Instead, they obey because pay, conscription, or a course of training has induced them to obey by rule. (Sometimes in fear for their lives, they abruptly reject the rule. The authority of the commanding officer then vanishes, and to control the soldiers he must resort to some ad hoc method of control, such as threatening to shoot a soldier who will not obey a command to move forward under fire.)

In government, the President and Congress obey decisions handed down by the Supreme Court, not because the Court has any specific method of control to enforce each decision, but because the president and Congress have accepted a rule of obedience to Court decisions on certain matters. Similarly, by rule, Congress accepts a presidential veto, members of the House obey orders of the Speaker of the House, and

[2]Sometimes a person chooses to follow a rule of obedience to another person even if that person has done nothing to induce him or her to do so.

members of congressional committees obey orders of the committee chairman. Control by rules of obedience operates everywhere in government, in high places and low.

Authority may be defined as: X has authority over Y if Y follows a rule to obey X.[3] If X controls Y by holding out in each specific decision some reward, threat, or physical constraint, X has control but not authority over Y. If X controls Y by persuading Y of the merit of a specific command, X has control but not authority over Y. But if X controls Y because Y has accepted a standing rule of obedience, then X has that particular form of control over Y which we call authority.

Authority is specific. Even so powerful a policy maker as the President of the United States has only limited authority. For example, he cannot remove Supreme Court justices. Nor does a top military commander have authority beyond specific assignment and is in many systems without authority over policy. In the United States, the president has authority to instruct the commander.

Authority, either voluntary or forced, is a concession from those who agree to obey. The rule that establishes authority governs the behavior of the person controlled, not of the controller. A legislative leader, for example, has no authority over legislators until they decide to follow, because coerced, because of custom, or for whatever reason, a rule of obedience.

It is fragile. A regime can be abruptly toppled if enough activists in the play of power simply withdraw their grants of obedience. A group of colonels can remove a Latin American president in minutes by their decision to withdraw a rule of obedience. An American president can easily lose the informal authority granted him by Congress in an earlier period of enthusiasm.

It is conceded for a variety of reasons. Since "authority" refers to a rule, what we said above about why people obey rules also explains why people grant authority. As with other rules, in some circumstances authority is often voluntarily conceded because people find it convenient to have

[3]Some social scientists define authority differently: for example Robert A. Dahl, *Modern Political Analysis,* 2nd ed. (Englewood Cliffs, N.J.: Prentice-Hall, Inc., 1970), chapter 3. They say: X has authority over Y if Y acknowledges the legitimacy of X's control over Y. Or X has authority over Y if Y acknowledges an obligation to obey X. There is no point in quarreling over the difference in definition. That Y's accepting such a rule logically implies that Y concedes legitimacy to X's control is an allegation on which we need not take a position. Many German citizens who abhorred Nazism accepted a rule of obedience to the Nazi government. It seems unnecessary for our purposes to ask whether in some sense or other that means that they did or did not concede legitimacy to their rulers. We shall say that they conceded authority to their rulers if they accepted a rule of obedience, as most of them did.

someone give orders. We have already said, however, that people may agree to a rule of obedience because they have been threatened, terrorized, persuaded, paid, favored in other ways—for various reasons. As we have said, authority is created by the use of any of all possible methods of control to induce a rule of obedience. The distinctive character of authority comes not from the methods of control that establish it but from the use of these methods to extract a rule of obedience rather than to achieve ad hoc control on each occasion.

Authority stands as the bedrock of policy making, because it stands as the bedrock of government itself. One can define the policy makers as those participants in the play of power with authority over policy. The distinction between those who hold authority and those who obey it— who follow a rule of obedience—specifies a fundamental feature of the architecture of policy making. If rules regulate the play of power, the key rule is the rule of obedience establishing authority.

The Efficiency of Authority
One understands authority best through appreciation of some of its great advantages as a method of control in the play of power. If one or a few persons can, by an occasional threat, bribe, persuasion, or other inducement, extract from other persons a rule of obedience, they can escape the endless, costly task of using these same methods whenever they desire a response. Once you induce me to accept a rule of obedience to you, you may control me on a thousand occasions without further lifting your finger. For this reason authority becomes an efficient method for large-scale feats of social control, feats otherwise impossible. Any lasting, broadly powered government depends on many wide-ranging rules of obedience and on the response by rule of subordinate to superior officials.

Although officials will sometimes find it difficult and expensive to establish their authority, once established it often reduces the marginal cost to them of exercising control to near zero. To establish the authority of government, for example, a dictator may need to assemble and deploy an army or a large police force. Or the dictator may have to finance a vast program of broadcasting and other propaganda to induce citizens to follow a rule of obedience. With success, however, the additional, incremental, or marginal cost of inducing responses to governmental orders may be extremely small. The dictator need only issue commands. When response is required—for example, when tax payments fall due—there need not be any specific enforcement, persuasion, or inducement. The previously established rule of obedience suffices; with only a few exceptions, the subjects will pay. For democratic governments too, once authority is established and occasionally renewed, the use of authority to exert control in particular situations often costs little in money, time, or energy.

Indirect Use of Authority

Authority operates as an even more important control over policy because, when A wants to influence policy by influencing certain decisions of B, yet lacks any authority over B, A can often use such authority as A possesses over someone else to achieve some control over B. This we shall call the indirect use of authority. Examples are familiar. In Latin America, a military commander often has no authority over the president. But, because he has authority over the army sufficient to depose the president if he wishes, he can compel the president to follow certain policies or abstain from them. Or a public works director in an American municipality uses his or her hiring authority to build up a following who will vote as he or she wishes even though the director has no authority over how they vote. With that influence over votes, he or she can influence the mayor, despite having no authority over him or her. Any person with authority can use it indirectly. A grant of authority in one's hands always bestows a greater control over policy than the grant ostensibly allows.

Authority as a Base for Persuasion and Exchange

Authority and persuasion. To some extent persuasion itself rests on authority. The head of government and other persons in positions of great authority can command audiences easily through the media. In some systems, the potential of persuasion as a source of control over policy is recognized by forbidding large audiences to anyone except those in authority.

Authority and exchange. Among policy makers, most of the benefits that any can offer in exchange depend on his or her authority. For example, through authority a legislator can offer a vote, as in legislative vote trading. Or a high-level bureaucrat may have authority over a decision potentially beneficial to another policy maker and can offer to trade favors. Authority and exchange closely interwine. Perhaps the most common, indirect use of authority takes the form of a benefit in exchange, as, for example, in job offers to attract a following.

Authority and money. The exchange of money also often depends on authority. Rules of private property regulate the distribution of wealth, which determines who can most influence policy through spending. The use of money by public officials to influence other people, as when a mayor or city boss builds a loyal coterie of supporters by offering them and their relatives jobs in public construction projects, rests on the authority granted to the official to disburse public monies, an authority that the ordinary citizen does not possess. Another flow of money in politics comes from business enterprises through the authority of business executives to spend corporate income.

That authority intertwines with persuasion and exchange often obscures our perception of just how people achieve control in various situations. We can best understand interaction and control in the play of power to the extent that we can perceive not a jumble of controls but a combination of persuasion, exchange, and authority, along with other, less important methods.

MUTUAL CONTROL AND ADJUSTMENT

Whether exerted through persuasion, exchange, or authority, controls in the play of power in policy making run in all directions. Not ranged in wholly hierarchical order, with control moving exclusively from top to bottom, all participants control each other down the hierarchy, up the hierarchy, and across it at each level with mutual control over each other and a consequent mutual adjustment to each other. Persuasion clearly moves in all directions. So do political favors and threats. Money too enters the system at many points. Authority itself does not simply enforce a top-to-bottom control of policy but falls into patterns of reciprocal control to some degree. Peron, Khrushchev, Diem, Allende, and Nixon —like Chiang Kai-shek, Farouk, Maximilian, and Julius Caesar—were all brought down by subordinate authorities who indirectly used their authority to remove or execute their ostensible hierarchical superiors. Even highly authoritarian systems with conspicuous dominant leaders make policies through mutual control and adjustment. Despite Hitler's extraordinary powers, Nazi policy was subject to a constant tug-of-war between policy-making groups whose composition varied from time to time.[4]

Almost everyone knows that a good deal of political bargaining goes on in government. In partisan analysis, when two participants debate with each other, we may say they engage in bargaining. Usually, however, the term "bargaining" implies a trading of contingent benefits, payments, or favors. So defined, "bargaining" denotes any one of the several forms of exchange just identified. Some people also include in their concept of bargaining an exchange of threats.

Mutual control and adjustment rests on much more than bargaining. The head of the Department of Transportation and his counterparts in the Department of Energy, in the Office of Management and Budget, and in the Treasury inevitably will be locked into mutual adjustment even if they never bargain with each other. The transportation secretary knows that his policies must depend on energy and financial resources available. He also realizes that these policies will affect energy availabilities. Simi-

[4]Karl D. Bracher, *The German Dictatorship* (New York: Praeger Publishers, 1970.).

larly, the energy secretary knows that what he can do is affected by and affects transport policy. He also knows that Budget and Treasury have certain authority over him. And Budget and Treasury know that their legal authority over finance cannot be exercised effectively except in cooperation with the heads of all the major departments and the chief executive. So all tread warily, all try to avoid policies certain to stir the strong objection of the others, all look for interests that all can share so that each can pursue his desired policies without resistance from the others, and all store money in the bank by doing favors for others when possible. All this mutual adjustment can occur without a word between them, let alone any bargaining.

*   *   *   *   *   *

The description of the play of power outlined in this chapter encompasses only the most universal and fundamental features of all political systems: the distinction between policy makers and ordinary citizens; the dependence of the play on rules; the methods by which people control each other in policy making, especially the methods of persuasion, exchange, and authority; and mutual adjustment among participants in the play. Democratic policy making embraces certain additional distinctive characteristics, to which we now can turn.

CHAPTER SEVEN

DEMOCRACY IN THE PLAY OF POWER

In some political systems a special set of effective rules in the play of power prescribe that certain key officials shall be chosen and removed by a counting of citizen preferences for competing candidates. These rules depend on others such as those supporting free speech and assembly and the broad eligibility of citizens to run for electoral office. Special rules also establish the authority of elected officials over other officials, including the authority to appoint and remove them.[1] When all these rules operate in a system, we call it a democracy.

These democratic rules greatly affect the play of power in policy making. In various familiar ways they broadly disperse control over policy. Almost every adult can participate in choosing top policy-making officials through the vote, or can become a candidate. Every person enjoys some freedom to express opinions about politics to others, including officials. A large number of persons make careers out of participating in the play of power: legislators, interest-group leaders, party leaders and activists, newspaper columnists, candidates for office, public relations specialists, pollsters, and other political "technicians" working for candidates and officials.

Democratic rules, and indeed those of liberal constitutional systems that preceded the establishment of democracy, also prohibit some of the harshest forms of in-fighting among officials and aspirants to office. Although broken from time to time, the rules forbid leaders to exile or to silence each other. They also curb such practices as character assassina-

---

[1]We shall refer to a system in which such rules are effective as a democracy, as illustrated by the governments of Western Europe and North America. For the moment, we leave open the question of whether they are "really" very democratic.

tion, although they apply only loosely to such points. Democratic rules largely limit struggles among leaders to softer kinds of mutual contention. Leaders consequently seek each other's support by doing each other political favors, as in vote trading. Or they band together in political parties, using joint funds and efforts in mutually helpful ways. They threaten each other not with loss of life but with refusals to cooperate, with public criticism, with withdrawal of funds, and with the possibility that they will use their authority (for instance, as civil servants or legislators) to frustrate opponents. Even the typical forms of rule breaking are distinctively less harsh: ballot stuffing, for example, rather than coup d'etat.

The dependence of elected officials on votes and of appointed officials on the favor of elected officials makes the pursuit of the vote central to democratic politics. This pursuit requires, among other things, large expenditures of money to reach the voter through print and broadcasting, to maintain campaign organizations, to cultivate local political and opinion leaders, and to ring doorbells. Democratic politics remains as dependent on money as nondemocratic politics does. More precisely, it depends on persons, business enterprises, and other institutions with large sums to put into politics.

THE SMALL NUMBER OF POLICY MAKERS

The number of policy makers, though enlarged by democratic rules, as when a military clique gives way to a legislature of several hundred members, remains tiny when compared to the citizenry as a whole. Immediate policy making remains in the hands of an elected elite and their appointees. In a few countries—Switzerland, for example—citizens vote directly on a small amount of legislation. In many American states, citizens vote on constitutional amendments and in some states on a small amount of legislation. In some towns, citizens vote directly on the budget. But direct participation in policy decisions through voting remains impossible for all but a few decisions. Policy making requires too many decisions. When thousands of issues await decision, even simple ones cannot be decided by voting. Each U.S. Congress passes between six hundred and one thousand bills and turns down thousands more. Moreover, one policy decision may run beyond the time and competence that the citizen can bring to it. In short, although democratic rules enlarge participation, they still require a policy-making elite.

If citizens usually exercise direct control only over the selection of an elite who will occupy top policy-making positions, then does democracy actually give the citizens much effective control over policy? Disagreement on the answer is based partly on factual questions, such as whether voters choose a candidate by his or her policies or by personality or charisma. It also is based on normative questions about what counts most for popular control: for example, legislators who will passively do exactly what their constituents want or those who will try to educate their constituents and will therefore at least occasionally thwart them. Much of the rest of this book provides information that will help answer the question of whether democracy gives the citizen effective control over policy making.

NEW COMPLICATIONS IN POLICY MAKING

Simply because of the larger numbers of policy makers in a democracy compared to a nondemocratic system, democracy brings about new difficulties in policy making. Under democratic rules, the very number of policy makers, although it remains a tiny minority of the citizenry, requires many new governmental arrangements for cooperation through mutual adjustment. Tying all the policy makers to the wishes of voting citizens further complicates this process, as do the activities of interest-group and party leaders characteristic of democracy.

Other things being equal, these complications decrease the predictability with which any one policy maker can expect his or her actions to achieve any specific intended effects. They also increase the difficulty of assigning responsibility to any particular participants. Democratic rules, in short, often turn small systems of clique or oligarchy into huge pluralistic policy-making systems difficult to understand, to design for predictable outputs, and to participate in effectively. The gains from democracy are bought at a cost.

The frequent sense of impotence that troubles the ordinary citizen may derive partly from these and other complications of democracy. Democratic rules give him or her the vote and thus lift expectations. But they also give the vote to millions of other citizens and thus render a single vote almost powerless.

The Complications of Liberty

One family of complications in democratic policy making arises out of a deliberately created division and overlapping of authority that requires various participants in policy making to specialize in different functions, on the one hand, and to interfere with each other, on the other hand. Both President and Congress, for example, play specialized roles. But the President sometimes vetoes acts of Congress, and Congress sometimes refuses the President funds for his assigned functions. The familiar term "separation of powers" refers to such specialization through division of authority, and "checks and balances" refers to mutual interference through overlapping authority.

If designers of constitutional and democratic systems had singularly attended to the policy-making process, presumably these pluralist complications would not have been introduced. But they had something else in mind—curbing the arbitrary power of rulers. As noted in chapter 1, they wanted liberty, not popular control of policy making. Opponents of royal power first introduced the separation of powers, as well as checks and balances, to disperse authority to the nobility, aristocracy, and an emerging middle class who could use it to protect their liberties. Subsequently, in the name of democracy, authority has been dispersed to the citizens to protect their liberties.

These and other libertarian rules complicate policy making in many ways. Policy making through two legislative houses rather than one, for example, makes it difficult to carry through any policy program. It also is complicated by presidential and gubernatorial veto powers, as well as by the two-thirds rule for overriding presidential or gubernatorial vetoes. Although much circumvented, the Electoral College is another device that obstructs a more simple popular control, as does the assignment of two senators to each state regardless of population. The division of authority between state and national government also often throws obstruction in the way. All of these devices hark back to the intention to curb a potential overconcentration of authority in government, thus safeguarding the inalienable rights celebrated in the Declaration of Independence. Though a laudable intention, it differs from and conflicts with the intention to provide instruments for popular control over policy making.

ORGANIZING AND COORDINATING

The complexities of democratic policy making call for special methods of organization and coordination through mutual adjustment not anticipated in constitutional design.

In the Legislature

Any one legislator has to resolve more conflicts and cooperate with more colleagues than he or she can ever engage in sustained discussion. In one year in the House of Representatives, nearly ten thousand bills and over fifteen hundred resolutions were introduced, each calling for a decision. Four hundred and thirty-five members cannot handle such a flow without special arrangements. Their policy making therefore requires additional organizational machinery; they need a government within a government.

The congressional committee system serves as one of the major devices for cooperation. Although a parliamentary system like that of the United Kingdom delegates all major policy-making responsibility to one committee—the cabinet—the American system delegates it to a plurality of policy-machine legislative committees.[2] The House operates through

---

[2]Extended analysis and detail on the congressional committee system is in Richard F. Fenno, Jr., *Congressmen in Committees* (Boston: Little, Brown & Co., 1973)

about twenty standing committees, most of them divided into largely autonomous subcommittees, thirteen for the Committee on Appropriations. Except for the powerful committees on Rules, Appropriations, and Ways and Means, most committees cover a policy area: for example, Armed Services, Education and Labor, and Agriculture. In the Senate, committees also beget subcommittees, their divisions roughly paralleling those of the House.

Both the House and the Senate in large part delegate policy decisions to the committees. With some exceptions, legislation comes to the floor of the House or Senate only after a committee has considered it and has made a recommendation. Only a small fraction of the thousands of bills introduced in Congress each year ever survive the committees. Of the bills that do, the House and the Senate more often than not follow committee recommendations or amend the bills only in minor ways.

The committees, each with a chair who is granted substantial authority, can be thought of as a group of independent "little legislatures" bound together by their common obligation to the members of the House and Senate as a whole. They are not tied together by any "super" committees. Nor do they join as a coordinating body, steering committee, committee of committees, or legislative cabinet. Each committee, and in many cases, each subcommittee, practices a striking degree of autonomy.

Executive Leadership in Policy Making

The same need for organization, delegation, specialization, and leadership that drives Congress to create a committee system, drives it to seek executive leadership in initiating policies. Believing that it needs even more leadership than the autonomous committees and their respective chairs provide, it turns to the President.

As government takes on new functions over the years, some of them, like monetary management, foreign aid, and space exploration, pose problems beyond the competence and time that Congress can bring to their solution. In addition, Congress has explicitly loaded onto the President an enlarged policy-making authority by requiring him to recommend to Congress a budget of proposed expenditures for each year. Roughly eighty percent of the bills enacted into law now originate in the executive branch; and the President now largely determines the policy-making agenda of Congress, although less so than a British prime minister or cabinet does for Parliament.

Constitutional grants of specific authority to the President in the American system make him more powerful than any other official. The Constitution grants him broader powers of appointment than any other official has and empowers him to oversee the executive branch,[3] com-

---

[3]Hence, as the federal bureaucracy grows (from a quarter of a million civilian employees in 1901 to 3 million today), the president's tasks and powers grow.

mand the military, supervise diplomatic negotiations, and veto congressional legislation. When Congress also grants him leadership in policy making, the President comes to be almost "king and prime minister rolled into one."[4]

The increase in presidential power in policy making stems partly from the president's own initiatives. He uses his authority indirectly to intervene in policy matters beyond the direct scope of his authority. For example, his authority over patronage, appropriations and publicity, and other favors he can grant, all can be used indirectly. No aspect of policy making lies beyond his reach.[5]

Moreover, democratic systems require inventive leadership for the management of conflict among the many interests free to press their demands in such systems. In particular, they require leadership with the skills in partisan analysis identified at the conclusion of chapter 4, leadership capable of restructuring political controversy, finding common interests among groups otherwise in contention, and hence moving the nation from profitless controversies to new vision and action. That kind of leadership can spring from either house of Congress or, for that matter, from anywhere in the system. The obligation and opportunities to provide it, however, both rest especially on the President. Some presidents try to respond and in so doing seek a place in history.

Legislative Parties

Compared to British parliamentary politics, American political parties shape policy only weakly in Congress. Members elected on the same party ticket, however, will choose committee chairs and the Speaker of the House. They will also bind themselves, at least loosely, together in a caucus in each House, will elect from among themselves such officers as the party leader and party whip, and will organize various party committees to arrange cooperation among party members.[6] Without such cooperation, if each member were to go his or her own way, no member could effect any policy.

Parties exert even more influence on policy. Once members of Congress or state legislators concede any significant authority to their party leaders, the leaders can strengthen their control by indirect use of

---

[4]For an extended analysis of the presidency and of the President's relations with Congress, see Thomas E. Cronin and Texford G. Tugwell, eds., *The Presidency Reappraised*, 2nd ed. (New York: Praeger Publishers, 1977): Stephen J. Wayne, *The Legislative Presidency* (New York: Harper & Row, Publishers, 1978), and George C. Edwards III, *Presidential Influence in Congress* (San Francisco: W. H. Freeman & Co., 1979).

[5]John F. Manley, "Presidential Power and White House Lobbying," *Political Science Quarterly*, 93 (Summer 1978).

[6]William J. Keefe and Morris S. Ogul, *The American Legislative Process*, 3rd ed. (Englewood Cliffs, N.J.: Prentice-Hall, Inc., 1973), chapter 9; and Malcolm E. Jewell and Samuel C. Patterson, *The Legislative Process in the United States*, 2nd ed. (New York: Random House, 1973), chapter 8 and *passim*.

their authority. They can sometimes hold a legislator to a party program by threatening to deny him or her a leadership role in the legislature. They can win further authority through their power to offer a variety of reciprocal favors.[7] As legislators testify, "They can do a lot towards seeing whether your bill will get on the calendar and pushing the hearings along," or: "You get better committee assignments, and you get appointed to interim committees and all kinds of easy assignments like that," and "If you stick with the party, they'll take care of you. Get you a job after defeat." Every legislator's admitted need for information and advice points to still another reason for following party leadership on policy. No legislator can be well informed on any but a small number of issues. "If you are in doubt, right or wrong, follow the party—and there's always something that's in doubt."[8]

Self-Selected Special Roles in Policy Making

The complexities of democratic government open up a broad range of choice for legislators as to how they will play their roles in the play of power in policy making. If they care little about re-election, their options become extremely broad. If their principal objective is to be re-elected, more commonly the case, the constraints on them still leave broad options. They need not pursue those policies favored by their constituents. Instead, they may seek the favor of their constituents by winning benefits, for example, construction projects—for their district or state. Legislators increasingly do just that. They may go so far as to specialize in claiming credit for such benefits without actually doing much to win them. Another option is to take conspicuous stands on policy issues, while not actually working for any policy.[9] On the policy choices they actually make, they will face, one way or another, the classical choice of options: working for those policies wanted by their constituents or for those policies judged best by the legislator.[10] Similar alternatives are open to bureaucrats, judges, and other policy makers.

Implications for Popular Control

Given all these arrangements for legislative organization, executive leadership, legislative parties, and given the options open to policy makers, no straightforward relation holds between what citizens want and the

[7]Randall B. Ripley, *Congress* (New York: W. W. Norton & Co., Inc., 1975), pp. 126–45.

[8]The quotations from Congress are in John C. Wahlke and others, *The Legislative System* (New York: John Wiley and Sons, Inc., 1962), pp. 366–67.

[9]These various possibilities are documented and discussed in David Mayhew, *Congress: The Electoral Connection* (New Haven, Conn.: Yale University Press, 1974).

[10]On the elected official's different understandings of his or her role, see Malcolm E. Jewell and Samuel C. Patterson, *The Legislative Process in the United States,* 2nd ed. (New York: Random House, 1973), pp. 407–10. For the United Kingdom see Samuel H. Beer, *British Politics in the Collectivist Age* (New York: Alfred A. Knopf, Inc. 1966).

policies they get. How elected officials will make policy depends on the structure of rules, authority relations, procedures, and organizations mediating between an elected official and the effect he or she exerts on policy. Moreover, since policy makers usually design these arrangements for their own convenience rather than to increase the effectiveness of popular control, many of them obstruct popular control. The policy makers who design them often intend just that: to insulate themselves to some degree from the demands of the citizenry. Similarly, policy makers choose among alternative possible roles, not to effect popular control but to suit their own needs. Despite long-standing complaints brought by voters against congressional procedures, its internal organization suits Congress itself well enough.[11]

Although such a state of affairs in the play of power does not emasculate democracy, it fails to correspond closely with most democratic models of citizen control over policy making. The rules of democracy throw important powers and liberties into the citizen's hands, but confer only a loose control over policy.

We are not so naive as to ask, "Who makes automobiles in the United States?" unless we intend to be satisfied with the name of a corporation. Clearly we do not expect one or a few persons, or kinds of persons, to be named. We know that thousands of people directly engage, millions indirectly, in making cars. Workers make cars. Managers do, too. And so do machines, builders of the machines, suppliers of parts, makers of parts, bookkeepers, custodians, printers, and oil drillers whose oil makes plastics. We are sophisticated enough to drop the "who" question about automobiles and ask instead about the complex system from which a product emerges through contributions of millions of people interacting with each other. We want to work toward a similar understanding of how policies are made. Our outline of the already complex democratic play of power now requires us to place bureaucrats, business managers, and interest groups in the policy-making process.

[11]David Mayhew, *Congress: The Electoral Connection*, (New Haven, Conn.: Yale University Press, 1974) pp. 81–82.

CHAPTER EIGHT

IMPLEMENTATION AND BUREAUCRATIC POLITICS

The complexities of the play of power in policy making—its indirections, unpredictabilities, frustrations, reversals, and inevitable partial failures—multiply in policy implementation. Normally the function of the administrative branch, or bureaucracy, implementation is the largest part of government if measured by the people engaged in it or by the funds spent on it. Ninety-eight of every hundred U.S. government employees work in the bureaucracy. The mere size of the government's efforts at administrating or implementing of policy poses staggering problems of resolving conflict and of arranging cooperation. Many and diverse agencies of implementation constantly collide with each other or discover overlapping responsibilities that open up possibilities for cooperation, surveillance, or mutual obstruction. Fragmentation of administrative authority in the United States also aggravates the problems. In educational policy, for example, one recent count showed nine different departments and twenty independent agencies at work. Among other tasks, the units regulate roughly fifteen thousand local school districts.

In principle and perhaps sometimes in fact, the administration or implementation of policy is divided into two kinds of activities, a point worth mentioning only to permit us to ignore one and turn our attention to the other. In principle some administrative acts merely implement a prior policy decision. If so, we can forget them as not part of policy making. Most, perhaps all, administrative acts make or change policy in the process of trying to implement it. For all such acts we must analyze implementation as part of policy-making.

Take, for example, the simplest kind of policy. The governor instructs the state police to enforce a fifty-five miles-per-hour highway speed limit. The state police commissioner then must decide such questions as whether to allow motorists a five or ten miles-per-hour leeway over the fifty-five or none at all, whether to concentrate enforcement on the state's main highways or on the more dangerous two-lane secondary highways, and whether to arrest a few violators or draw officers from other tasks in order to make a large number of arrests. Given the commissioner's policy decision, each patrol officer must subsequently decide whether to hold tightly to or to interpret loosely the commissioner's decision on the five or ten miles-per-hour leeway. Despite the governor's decision, the state's actual operative policy may be to arrest a small proportion of drivers driving over seventy miles-per-hour on secondary highways. A fuller statement of state policy would have to take account also of how judges handled specific cases after arrest. Perhaps the operative policy of the state also levies heavier fines on disreputable-looking drivers than on more respectable-looking citizens.[1]

IMPLEMENTATION AS POLICY MAKING

Implementation always makes or changes policy in some degree. Let us note the various ways in which an ostensible policy in the form, say, of a new piece of legislation or an executive order, undergoes significant alteration at the hands of administrators.[2]

Incomplete Specification of the Ostensible Policy. No ostensible policy makers can fully formulate their policy, and few attempt it. They know they cannot write a law, for example, that covers all contingencies, all possible cases. They instead ask or allow the administrator to design large elements of the policy that they have only begun to design. Congress instructs, for example, the Federal Communications Commission to license television stations for "public convenience and necessity." Clearly it issued an imprecise policy statement because it did not want to take on the job of deciding licensing policy in any but the vaguest way.

Imprecision may also arise either from haste or from the failure of legislation to specify. Either leaves more policy-making authority in the bureaucracy than the legislature may have intended. An example is federal grants to states to enlarge child-health programs. Because the grants failed to specify which programs are eligible, Congress in fact permitted the bureaucracy to distribute the funds in such a way as to achieve little

---

[1]Some people might say that the governor's declaration constitutes policy; all else is practice rather than policy. In this book, since we want to understand how governments come to do what they do, we use the term "policy" to denote what is actually done. Moreover, many legislative or executive acts are designed to compel administrators formally to formulate policy on points on which a vague legislative or executive policy is silent.

[2]The list that follows is, in varying versions, familiar in the literature. For another version, for example, see George C. Edwards III and Ira Sharkansky, *The Policy Predicament* (San Francisco: W. H. Freeman and Company, 1978), chapter 10.

more than a transfer of existing programs from state to federal funds, largely negating the professed congressional policy of improving health care.

Conflicting Criteria for Application.   Whenever policy makers specify, as they often must, the various conflicting criteria which they intend to govern the application of a policy, policy making falls in some degree into the administrator's hands. For example, a minimum wage law might require wage setting according to two criteria: cost of living and industry's ability to pay. Although the two constitute a reasonable set of guidelines, they point in opposite directions, the one often calling for higher wages when the other calls for lower. In specifying the two, the legislature may or may not realize that it leaves their reconciliation, thus a significant part of the actual determination of policy, in the hands of the administrator.

Multiple conflicting criteria are a universal phenomenon in policy implementation, appearing also in areas far removed from ordinary policy implementation in democracies. In the Soviet Union, for example, it has long been acknowledged that a chronic deficiency in planning arises out of the degree of freedom that multiple criteria give to enterprise managers to set production policy for themselves. They are given orders to produce high outputs but at the same time to show a profit, to minimize costs, to conserve specified inputs, and to achieve certain product mixes. Since they cannot do all of these things, the managers have to make policy within broad limits for themselves.

Incentive Failures.   Administrative incentives to do as the ostensible policy requires are usually somewhat inadequate. The condition poses the classical difficulty of authority. In an authority system, those commanded will obey, but only partially and with some misdirection because of personal incentives conflicting with their rule of obedience. Everyone knows some of these obstructions: sometimes, for example, an administrator's desire to avoid hard work, sometimes his or her disinclination to take on the unpleasantness of enforcing policy, sometimes career ambitions deterring him or her from wishing to be associated with an unpopular policy, sometimes bribes accepted for not carrying through the assigned policy. The incentives that authority systems create—for example, pay, promotions, prestige—never replace but only supplement the incentives already governing the administrator's behavior. Often they do not add enough to gain control over his or her behavior. Presidents Roosevelt, Truman, and Kennedy all left a record of explicit complaint that presidential orders were often ignored or only feebly implemented. To a significant degree, policy turns out to be what the administrators choose to do, not what an ostensible policy decision declares.

Conflicting Directives.   Those implementing policy often receive conflicting policy instructions from more than one source. Although the stereotype of the bureaucrat may show him nicely positioned in a pyramid of superiors and subordinates taking orders from one and only one superior, most administrators take orders from more than one superior. President Kennedy ordered the removal of American missiles from Turkey. Other channels specified an American policy of support to NATO through cooperation with the Turks. Faced with conflicting policy directives, Department of Defense administrators themselves set actual policy, to leave the missiles in Turkey.[3]

Limited Competence.   Administrators sometimes do not know how to do what the policy requires them to do, as in the conspicuous example of drug abuse policy. Not knowing how to curb abuse, as policy directs them to do, administrators have experimented with a variety of policies of their own design, or have simply not acted. In difficult program areas, like improving the education of disadvantaged children, reducing urban blight, and stimulating the economic growth of Third-World countries, legislators will often feel compelled to inaugurate programs beyond anyone's competence. Faced with the impossibility of announced policy, administrators to some degree then set their own policy.

Inadequate Administrative Resources.   Administrators sometimes lack the authority and other necessary controls, including staff and funds, to carry out ostensible policy. Congress often authorizes programs without providing necessary funds. Funding is often inadequate because Congress has miscalculated requirements, or because it has vacillated on its commitment to the policy, or because it wants credit with some voters for the authorization and with other voters by withholding appropriations. Sometimes one Congress does not wish to finance what the preceding Congress has authorized. Again the administrator has to make policy to a degree by deciding to which activities the limited funds and staff will be assigned and how energetically this or that part of the policy will be pursued.

Administrators will often be pushed deeply into policy making, because they lack exclusive jurisdiction in the policy area and have to work out policy in interaction with other officials. Usually they lack it. The U.S. Office of Education has funds to allocate to schools for special educational programs. But local school boards, state education commissioners, and state education departments also control the schools. These groups can negate the Office of Education's policy most easily by divert-

[3]Morton H. Halperin, *Bureaucratic Politics and Foreign Politics* (Washington, D.C.: Brookings Institution, 1974), p. 245.

ing their own funds out of special education programs as fast as Office of Education's money moves in. In another example, the federal government undertakes an urban renewal project in cities. But local fire commissioners, city planners, city councils, mayors, building inspectors, state highway departments, courts, and others control what can be rehabilitated, demolished, and reconstructed. Each can make the others' policies impossible, and no policy except inaction can be established without cooperation among them. In these cases, no formal action by the federal government or by any of the other participants sets policy. It develops through mutual adjustment among all the participants, mostly administrators rather than ostensible policy makers.

For all these reasons, the conditions in which administrators are expected to implement policy compel them to join in the policy *making* process. We should also file a reminder that implementation additionally makes policy for the reason mentioned in chapter 5. Whenever, and that means almost always, policy making proceeds through trial-and-error, whenever next steps correct the inadequacies of a preceding step, implementation of each step in policy making becomes a principal source of feedback information for the next step. The record of implementation of earlier policies constantly pushes policy in new directions with new information.

BUREAUCRATIC POLITICS

If we could count all the policy-making acts of policy makers in any political system—attempts at persuasion, agreements reached, threats and promises made, authoritative commands given or received, and the like—we would find that, so defined, policy making rests overwhelmingly in the hands of the bureaucracy, leaving relatively few policies to be determined elsewhere. Although the executive, the legislature, and the judiciary set some of the most important policies, the bureaucracy sets most, including those of the highest importance. Policy emerges specifically in the mutual interactions of bureaucratic politics surveyed in this chapter.[4]

In bureaucratic politics, the bureaucrat works with the methods of control outlined earlier: chief among them, authority, exchange, persuasion and analysis. All of these controls are used both alone and in cooperation with other participants who find themselves in agreement on at least some issues. On some issues the bureaucrat forms a close alliance with other administrators. On some issues he or she may have the support of important high-level administrators, heads of departments, or the Presi-

---

[4]On bureaucratic politics, see Aaron Wildavsky and Jeffrey L. Pressman, *Implementation* (Berkeley: University of California Press, 1973) and Francis E. Rourke, *Bureaucracy, Politics and Public Policy* (Boston: Little, Brown & Co., 1969).

dent. As a long-standing major practice in bureaucratic politics, he or she will often ally with an interest group: for example, the U.S. Department of Agriculture allies itself with the American Farm Bureau Federation, and the Office of Education with the National Education Association. Often a legislative committee in the same policy area joins the alliance.

Both the two-way and the three-way alliance often constitute a challenge to effective policy control by the legislature as a whole, a dangerous challenge in the eyes of some observers.[5] Many people see an even larger problem: the fragmentation of the policy-making authority characterizing American policy making, which bureaucratic politics exacerbates. They see it as a challenge to both rational policy making and democratic control. A necessary division of labor in policy making, they believe, degenerates into an excessive fragmentation of responsibility.

In bureaucratic politics, state highway departments illustrate the problem. They want to build highways with little regard for other interests and values. They can do so because excellently financed by state gasoline taxes and enthusiastically supported by construction contractors, cement manufacturers, construction workers' unions, and others who profit from their large expenditures. Administrators with responsibilities for, say, urban development, recreational areas, or zoning consequently find highway departments difficult to deal with; and even the legislative and the federal government cannot cope with their independence.

Opinions differ about when fragmentation creates a useful division of labor and when it goes too far. When Congress considered the Occupational Health and Safety Act, some policy makers and their allies wanted key powers of enforcement to be given to the Department of Labor on the supposition that it would sympathize with labor. Others wanted to keep those powers out of the department for the same reason. The resulting compromise legislation created a questionable degree of fragmentation. It granted the Department of Labor authority to set and enforce standards. But appeals go to an independent commission. And to the Department of Health, Education, and Welfare, the legislation assigned research on health standards for the use of the Department of Labor and the commission.[6]

In the democratic play of power, the endless intricacies of bureaucratic policy making mix with those of presidential, congressional, and judicial policy making, as illustrated in policy in the 1970s on desegregation. In 1969 in *Alexander* v. *Holmes,* the Supreme Court demanded speedier administrative implementation of the desegregation policy it had first set in 1954 in its historic *Brown* v. *The Board of Education* desegre-

---

[5]See Theodore J. Lowi, *The End of Liberalism* (New York: W. W. Norton & Co., Inc., 1969).

[6]James E. Anderson, *Public Policy Making* (New York: Praeger Publishers, 1975), p. 105.

gation decision. President Nixon resisted the Court by dragging his heels on enforcement of desegregation; he refused, for example, to withhold funds from segregated schools, thus surrendering his principal means of enforcement. Congress also threw various new obstacles in the path of busing. Following two new Nixon appointments, the Court itself appeared to draw back from the vigorous enforcement demanded in 1969. State and local educational officials delayed in complying with the law, often misrepresenting their local policies to federal officials. In various inconspicuous ways these officials reinforced on some fronts the segregation they abandoned on others. Despite the apparent clarity of policy in *Alexander* v. *Holmes,* the actual policy result produced a very small movement toward desegregation.[7] No one made such a policy, but it happened. It can be praised by referring to its sensitivity to many interests and values, or condemned for failing to advance the cause of desegregation.

POLICY ANALYSIS AND ADVICE IN THE BUREAUCRACY

Implementation aside, we finally must acknowledge that administrators and bureaucrats perform another major role in policy making. At the higher levels, they serve as the principal immediate source of analysis and advice for ostensible policy makers. In the British system, every elected official explicitly recognizes that, while he or she may come and go, the civil service steadily proceeds to turn out policy studies and recommendations for their elected chiefs. The official understands that on most policy issues, elected officials can give only a general direction and loose supervision to policy makers in the civil service. Although in the American system, elected officials exert a closer, more direct influence on policy, even in the United States they lean heavily on the upper levels of the civil service for policy information and advice.

The extent of their dependence is indicated by an otherwise inexplicable characteristic of the emerging field of policy analysis in political science. Although one might expect that the study of policy analysis would belong to the study of the legislature, in fact it is associated in political science with the study of public administration. As academic specialties, policy analysis and the study of administration have largely merged. Insofar as various forms of policy analysis like systems analysis or cost-benefit studies arise in the American government, they usually do so in the administrative services.

[7]For a brief, documented summary of the specific developments on desegregation in the 1970s, see Ira Sharkansky and Donald VanMeter, *Policy and Politics in American Governments* (New York: McGraw-Hill Book Co., 1975), chapter 2.

CHAPTER NINE

THE PRIVILEGED POSITION OF BUSINESS IN POLICY MAKING

For reasons still not fully understood, no national democracy has ever taken root except in societies with a private enterprise market system. So far in history, a private enterprise market economy seems to be a requisite of democracy. The reverse is not true: many private enterprise market systems exist in the absence of democracy, as in Pakistan, Indonesia, Nigeria, Iran, and dozens of other countries.

So far as we can understand the reasons for democracy's dependence on the market, they turn on the association already noted between democracy and certain forms of liberty. To establish and protect their desired liberty to trade, operate businesses, and accumulate wealth, people have had to curb the authority of the state. They have insisted on basic civil liberties including, at least for people of property, the right to vote. The civil liberties so far have never flourished in any nation-state except in connection with liberties to participate relatively freely in market life and in private profit seeking. Democracy, wherever it develops, depends on these basic civil liberties.[1]

From the association of market, private enterprise, and democracy come consequences for the policy-making process. We shall try to trace the consequences, taking into account that they are not limited to the United States.

[1]For further discussion, see Charles E. Lindblom, *Politics and Markets* (New York: Basic Books, 1977), chapter 12. The "people's democracies" of the communist world, which do not practice rotation of top officials through citizen election, are not included in what we here call democracy.

TWO SETS OF PUBLIC OFFICIALS

Market systems require a second set of "public officials" and thus another elite. They are business managers, especially corporate executives, who discharge major public functions, although not as government officials. They, rather than government officials, undertake many of the main organizational tasks of society: organizing the labor force, allocating the nation's resources, developing the nation's investment program, and of course, undertaking the specific critical tasks of producing electric power, transportation services, many forms of entertainment, insurance services, steel, housing, food, computers, newspapers, toys—the list is long.

These functions are public in several senses, even though they are not governmental. They matter to all members of society. Decisions about them loom as momentous as the decisions of most government officials. Employment, price level, and growth rate all depend on policies set within corporations by their executives. No one can say that their decisions are too inconsequential to be labeled public policy.[2] We would understand their "publicness" better if we noted that in some countries, China and the Soviet Union, for example, government officials make these decisions. They are seen as too important for private decisions. In all countries of the world, some of these decisions from time to time move into the jurisdiction of government.

The most fundamental inequality in policy making, between policy makers and ordinary citizens, is duplicated in the market system. There, no less than in government, a fundamental inequality separates a business elite from the great mass.[3]

BUSINESS CONTROL OVER GOVERNMENTAL POLICY MAKING

In this book, we wish to analyze governmental rather than market policy making. For our purpose, the significance of the business leadership role in the market is in a consequent unusual kind and degree of control over governmental policy making given to business. This control comes about because of the following specific sequence of reasons:

Many of the functions performed by business managers in the market are essential to society in that, if not performed, widespread discontent and—at an extreme—disorder would follow. Housing must be built, food processed, people and goods transported, factories built and oper-

---

[2]For an example of business "policy making" in the steel industry, in which corporate executives at their discretion make a major decision on employment and output for the economy, see U.S. Congress, Senate Committee on the Judiciary, Subcommittee on Antitrust and Monopoly, Hearing on Egon Sohmen's testimony in *Economic Concentration,* 90th Cong., 2nd sess., 1968, p. 3446.

[3]What we say is not denied by loose consumer control over business accomplished by consumer "voting" with dollars when they buy or refuse to buy.

ated, and jobs made available. If these and other similar activities falter, widespread distress will follow.

Government officials recognize this. They also know that widespread failure of business to perform these functions will bring down the government. A democratically elected government cannot expect to survive in the face of widespread or prolonged distress. Extreme economic disorganization would not just evict officials in power but also would overthrow the entire regime or form of government. Consequently, government policy makers show constant concern about business performance.

By the rules of the private enterprise market system, however, no one, not even governments, can command business managers to perform the functions assigned to them. Although governments can prohibit, they cannot positively command business managers to perform their functions. A business manager produces or offers jobs only if he or she voluntarily decides to do so.

How then can a government official be reasonably confident that managers will discharge their necessary functions? By making sure that they will find it advantageous to themselves to do so. They will perform only if induced by benefits, gains, or advantages offered them.

One might think that, because opportunities for profit lie about everywhere, business managers will certainly find inducement to perform their functions. Yet not even Adam Smith believed that they would inevitably do so if left to their own devices. In many parts of the world they do not, as in India, for example. They perform their functions only when governments develop and maintain business profitability through supporting policies. Historically, these policies have a variety of forms: subsidized transportation and banking facilities, outright cash subsidies, protected markets, low business taxes, military protection for foreign investments, strike breaking, employee training programs, research services, and construction and subsidized rental of plants and equipment. In addition are policies of according business people easy frequent consultation with government officials, as well as those conferring rights on their trade associations or on certain business leaders to veto certain governmental appointments. One should add to the list tariffs, minimum price maintenance, purchases of surpluses, sharing of costs of new technologies, as well as many routine services like weather reporting, mapping, and policing.[4] When, as in some countries of the world, governments in market systems have not developed sufficient supporting policies, their economies have lagged in growth or have relapsed into depression.

[4]For a long list of U.S. business subsidies, see Clair Wilcox, *Public Policy Toward Business,* 4th ed. (Homewood, Ill.: Irwin, 1971), chapter 33. On the variety of support policies, see Murray Weidenbaum, *The Modern Public Sector* (New York: Basic Books, 1969), especially the table on p. 137.

The conclusion follows. To induce business managers to perform, governments must give them not everything they ask for, but everything they need for sufficiently profitable operation. Policy making consequently comes under a special control by business: government officials must listen to business with special care; must find out what business needs even if it does not take the trouble to speak for itself; must give managers enough of what they need to motivate production, jobs, and growth; and must in so doing give them special rights of consultation and actual participation in the setting of policies.

In each of these ways, governments award to business managers a privileged position in the play of power in policy making. The privileged position goes so far as to require that government officials must often give business needs precedence over demands from citizens through electoral, party, and interest-group channels. Although neglect of business brings stagnation or unemployment, at great peril to officials in power, citizen and interest-group demands can often be evaded or deflected, given the looseness of popular control over officials, outlined in chapter 7.

The Range and Kinds of Control

Precisely which policies can business influence through its privileged position? The range or variety is without particular limit. Business managers will ask for more than they need and more than they expect to win. Whatever they want, government officials must consider. The test of what they actually need is in whether, if they fail to get it, slackened growth, restricted output, and unemployment will ensue. Drawing on his experience in Du Pont, a businessman observes that "the strength of the position of business and the weakness of the position of government is that government needs a strong economy just as much as business does, and the people need it and demand it even more."[5] A business lobbyist says, "Jobs, payroll, economic growth—this is awfully important. A Congressman reacts positively to anything that affects jobs, growth in his district."[6]

Sometimes business managers threaten dire consequences if government policy does not meet their demands. Usually, however, they do not do so; the government official becomes accustomed to exercising a solicitous concern for the needs of business. Officials have been as quick as corporate executives, for example, in wishing to soften and delay new policies on environmental protection, fearing the adverse consequences of proposed new policies on business profitability and economic conditions of the nation. As environmental concerns mounted, the President

---

[5]Harold Brayman, *Corporate Management in a World of Politics* (New York: McGraw-Hill Book Co., 1967), p. 57.
[6]"Business Lobbying," *Consumer Reports,* 43 (September 1978), p. 529.

established the National Industrial Pollution Control Council to allow business executives to communicate with the president "to help chart the route by which our cooperative ventures will follow." Similarly, out of concern that new consumer offices in various federal agencies might damage business, the President established the National Business Council for Consumer Affairs, again to allow business executives to communicate regularly with him.[7]

Notice that these examples of benefits to business fall into two categories. The largest category consists of substantive policies helpful to business—those on taxes, for example. The second category consists of arrangements allowing business people to share in policy making explicitly and directly, as when government allows business associations to veto regulatory appointments or when business advisory groups attach, as is common, to many government departments. For example, in one period studied, the White House asked for industry opinions on appointments to the Federal Trade Commission and to the Federal Communications Commission (but refused to hear consumer groups).[8]

Business people exercise control through persuasion, exchange, and authority. Their privileged frequent communication with government officials makes persuasion easier than for other citizens. Their control works, however, largely through various kinds of exchanges. Sometimes the exchange takes the form of a *quid pro quo:* a corporation agrees to locate in a town only after bargaining with the municipal government over tax concessions. Another example:

> Unless the British government agreed to provide massive aid to Chrysler's troubled British subsidiary, Riccardo (chairman of Chrysler) said, the company would be forced to shut down its five major plants in Britain and cashier its 25,000 employees there. . . . [Prime Minister] Wilson denounced the Riccardo ultimatum, angrily protesting that Chrysler had left the government "with a pistol at its head." But last week in a startling, if characteristically Wilsonian, about-face, the Prime Minister agreed to help out Chrysler after all.[9]

More often business managers strike no explicit bargain. Government instead offers a benefit in hopes of a response. For example, government officials are told, or they surmise for themselves, that new investments will lag unless interest rates decline. So the monetary authorities reduce the rates in hopes of a reciprocal increase in investment. No

[7]Mark Green and Peter Petkas, "Nixon's Industrial State," *New Republic,* 167 (September 1972), p. 19.
[8]George C. Edwards III and Ira Sharkansky, *The Policy Predicament* (San Francisco: W. H. Freeman & Co., 1978), p. 47.
[9]*Time,* December 29, 1975, p. 61.

corporation promises anything in return, and they may or may not respond.

Formal authority is sometimes conferred on managers and their organizations, as when government officials follow, as already noted, a rule that regulations or appointments require clearance by certain companies or associations.[10] As an observer of a British business association remarked on its participation in government policy making: "It looked and acted like a government department."[11] In the United States, a congressional committee said of business participation in the Business and Defense Services Administration: "In operation, the organization arrangements of BDSA have effected a virtual abdication of administrative responsibility on the part of the Government officials in charge of the Department of Commerce in that their actions in many instances are but the automatic approval of decisions already made outside the Government in business and industry."[12]

Control without Trying

That business people usually exercise control without any expenditure of attention or any deliberation deserves emphasis. They simply operate under circumstances in which both they and government officials know that continued performance depends on business indulgences, benefits, privileges, and incentives. As we have said, if government provides enough, they will perform well; if not, the economy will languish. Under those circumstances, government officials routinely and constantly attend to the needs of business. When President Carter first took office, newspapers were full of comments like the following: "Will he seek at the outset to gain the confidence of the business and financial community, or will he risk their disfavor by moving rapidly and perhaps radically to attack the economic and social ills he campaigned against?"[13] (One might add that subsequently the answer became clear.) And his advisor on appointments declared that the new president wanted a Secretary of the Treasury "who can verbalize the concerns of the financial community and *anticipate* the financial community's reaction to economic decisions he might take."[14]

[10]Louis A. Kohlmeier, *The Regulators* (New York: Harper & Row, Publishers, 1969), p. 49.

[11]Stephen Blank, *Industry and Government in Britain* (Lexington, Mass.: D. C. Heath and Co., 1973), pp. 67–70, 211.

[12]Grant McConnell, *Private Power and American Democracy* (New York: Alfred A. Knopf, Inc., 1967), p. 271.

[13]Quoted in Charles E. Lindblom, *Politics and Markets* (New York: Basic Books, 1977), p. 189.

[14]*Ibid.* Italics added.

Business Privilege as Unique

To no other large category of citizens do government policy makers grant similar influence on and participation in the making of governmental policy. No other large category of citizens plays a leadership role indispensable to government. Members and leaders of labor unions enjoy no comparable influence and participation, except for their ability to block wage-control policies by threat of widespread strikes. Although society needs labor, workers and their unions can acquire special influence like that of business only if they can, like business managers, withhold performance of their functions until they get what they want. Aside from temporary work stoppages, labor cannot do so because it needs wages more urgently than society needs its services. Unlike business performance, wage-earner performance does not threaten a recession if wage earners are dissatisfied. Their unions, unlike business enterprises, perform no functions widely thought essential to society. They operate largely for the benefit of their own members, unlike an enterprise providing a commodity or service for a large clientele. People do not depend on the decisions of union leaders to provide growth and job opportunities.

OTHER BUSINESS INFLUENCES ON POLICY MAKING

A hiatus remains in the argument. It looks as though two quite separate control processes operate on government officials: customary electoral controls (votes, interest groups) and business controls.[15] Do the two conflict? If so, what happens?

In the United States and Western Europe, some mechanism resolves the conflict, one must infer, since we have no evidence that business fails to get what it needs. In these democracies businesspeople are performing well enough to avoid intolerable unemployment and other economic disorder—evidence that they win the basic indulgences in public policy that they judge they must have. Perhaps electoral controls, then, are too weak to challenge business controls? Or electoral controls are somehow regulated, manipulated, or bent so that they support rather than conflict with business controls?

Although business modifies its demands somewhat to avoid collision with electoral demands on government, the principal reconciliation between the two control systems comes about by adjusting electoral

[15]In order to contrast business controls with popular controls through elections, interest groups, and parties, we shall refer to all of the latter as electoral controls, meaning that they stem from the authority and influence of the electorate.

controls to make them consistent with those of business. Businesspeople bend or bring electoral controls into line by themselves entering into interest-group, party, and other electoral activities and achieving disproportionate influence on them.

Business does not enter into these activities on a parity with other groups—consumer, labor, professional, and veterans' groups, among others. These other groups depend on electoral activity as their main source of influence over government. For business people, electoral activity merely supplements the controls they already exercise through their privileged position in government. They enter into electoral activities simply to strengthen their privileged position by bending electoral controls toward the policies they seek through their more important privileged controls. We have already noted that the looseness of electoral controls often permits officials to do what business wants in any case.[16] Consequently, business managers do not have to bend electoral controls very far.

Specifically, how do business managers bring electoral controls to support the privileged position of business?

Persuasion of Citizens

Business managers join with government officials to present business demands as reasonable. Most government officials, the President included, assure the citizenry of their own concern for "the needs of business" and in so doing teach the citizenry that, since business needs must be met for the sake of a sound economy, their own hands and the citizens' are tied. Business managers continually issue such warnings—their words passed on in news stories and editorial comment alike—as that high taxes will hurt investment and jobs—as indeed they often will— or that pollution control requirements on automobile engines will retard production —as again they often will. Government officials join easily in such persuasive exercises because, given the rules of a market system, many business demands ask nothing unreasonable and still others look reasonable. The ordinary citizen must agree to give business demands priority over his or her own, unless, as only a few seriously contemplate, he is willing to give up the market system and private enterprise.

Over many years, citizens are told that their own jobs and prosperity would be jeopardized by any of a variety of policies that citizens might want and might demand through electoral activity: higher taxes on business instead of on themselves, requiring businesses to undertake the expenses of making mines and factories safer,[17] requiring them to pay

---

[16]Chapter 12 will examine additional imperfections in electoral control.

[17]For decades, neither the mine workers nor the United Mine Workers, for example, dared press for enforcement of safety legislation for fear that jobs would be endangered.

compensation to employees injured on the job, regulation of misleading advertising, tighter controls over consumer fraud, control of industrial discharges that pollute waterways and blight the land, and, above all, through wage increases a significantly larger share of the national income for low paid workers.

Although on some of these points business people have yielded, even today they enjoy what by some standards are extraordinary tax favors, they operate unsafe factories and mines, they can legally misrepresent many of their products to consumers, they greatly pollute the environment (despite growing curbs); and the distribution of income and wealth remains largely unchanged. Some citizens will wisely or foolishly draw the conclusion that, if policies like these must be accepted because of business needs in a private enterprise market system, it would be better to dispense with the system.

That very few citizens draw such a conclusion can be explained largely by their tendency to think of private enterprise and democracy as inseparable, indeed their own liberties and private enterprise as inseparable. Businesspeople and government officials steadily reinforce this view. In so doing they can point to the historical dependence, that we have already noted, of democracy on private enterprise and market. The easy confusion of private enterprise, democracy, and nation itself appears in many declarations like that of a recent Secretary of Interior: "This is the year to wave the flag and wave the free enterprise flag."[18] A British industrial association similarly identifies the interests of the whole society with the interests of business in declaring it will oppose subversion of "the security of Britain in general and British industry in particular."[19] Businesses make it a point to put their executives in leadership positions in public-interest organizations like the Red Cross and the United Fund. It becomes difficult for a citizen to distinguish democracy from private enterprise, to consider the possibility that the latter may be an undemocratic element in the former, and to see that business demands obstruct the democratic demands of the citizen.

The persuasive efforts of business people and government officials tend to remove important issues from policy debate. On fundamental issues pertaining to the structure of government and economy, a barrage of persuasion teaches citizens to accept corporate autonomy, the existing distribution of wealth, the limited authority of employees in business management, and close consultation between business and government as fundamental virtues of the established order not to be challenged. Consequently, they do not become policy issues.

---

[18] *New York Times*, June 8, 1976, p. 51.
[19] A. A. Rogow, *The Labour Government and British Industry* (Ithaca, N.Y.: Cornell University Press. 1955), p. 146.

Other Electoral Activities

Business people do not limit their electoral efforts to public declarations, propoganda, and public relations. Because electoral demands may obstruct business demands, business people plunge into the whole range of political activity open to citizens in a democracy. They become the most active citizens, and their corporations often become the most active private political organizations. Individuals and corporations both contribute to campaign funds, put their own energies to work in political parties and interest groups, and organize to further the candidacies of persons favorable to them. In the words of a West German business representative, "This is not an alien world to the entrepreneur; it is his own. At stake for him is the leadership of the state."[20]

Business Advantage

Granting that through persuasion and their participation in electoral activities business managers would like to bring electoral demands around to support the demands they make on government by means of their privileged position, they might fail. That they largely succeed in the United States and many other countries follows from their four great advantages over all other groups.

Funds. Their first advantage lies in the funds available to them. No other interest group has comparable funds at its disposal; they dwarf union or other interest-group resources.[21] As an example of the disproportion, one form of business lobbying—programs to mobilize grassroots support among businesses all over the country behind initiatives undertaken by business group representatives in Washington—runs to about $1 billion per year in recent years, according to a congressional committee estimate. That amounts to more than a thousand times the combined total expenditures of the major consumer protection groups: the Consumer Federation of America, Ralph Nader's Congress Watch, and the National Consumers League. If one adds the budgets of Common Cause and environmental protection organizations to those of the three consumer groups, the grand total will rise to about $3 million, roughly three-tenths of one percent of the expenditure on the business grassroots campaign. Another single business organization for influencing policy, the Business Roundtable, has a budget of $2 million, more than the combined budgets of the consumer and environmental groups.[22]

[20]Quoted in Heinz Hartmann, *Authority and Organization in German Management* (Princeton N.J.: Princeton University Press, 1959), p. 229.

[21]For estimates, see Charles E. Lindblom, *Politics and Markets* (New York: Basic Books, 1977), pp. 194–96. See also David W. Adamany and George E. Agree, *Political Money* (Baltimore: Johns Hopkins University Press, 1975).

[22]"Business Lobbying," *Consumer Reports*, 43 (September 1978), pp. 526–29.

"Public" Sources of Funds.   A second advantage lies in the source of business funds for political activity. These funds do not come out of the income of those who offer them. Most interest groups must finance their work out of contributions from personal income, but business interest-group activity does not. A curious and extraordinary arrangement from some perspectives, democracies permit one category of citizens, business people, to finance their interest-group activity out of "public" funds—the receipts of business enterprises, especially the receipts of corporate enterprises.[23]

Available Organizations.   A third great advantage of businesspeople in politics is in their organizations, already functioning and ready. Every corporate enterprise constitutes an interest group, as does a small business in local politics. Ordinary citizens can organize political activity only if they are willing to pay a great price in time, energy, and money. Corporate executives pay no such great price. They do not need laboriously and expensively to assemble a team of political activists; they can use those already on the payroll. Business managers' use of their own enterprises as political organizations has come to be common practice in the democracies.[24]

Access.   The fourth great advantage of businesspeople in electoral politics derives from the ease of access to government officials they already enjoy because of their privileged position. Already engaged in routine and frequent discussion with government officials, already frequently called upon by officials for information and advice, when business people turn to interest-group and campaign activity, doors stand open for them, habits of consultation already established.

A Changing Relation of Business to Government Officials?

"The defender of American business had it pretty easy in 1955," says the magazine of the National Association of Manufacturers. "There were in those happy days no self-ordained public interest lobbyists to cope with; and the Eisenhower Administration in league with the conservative leadership of Congress championed the interests of business whenever those interests were threatened."[25] The nineteen-sixties and seventies, how-

---

[23]There are legal restrictions on corporate contributions to campaign funds. They are widely evaded. Many corporations also take the legal route of asking their executive personnel to make personal campaign contributions, which are legal. The corporation can adjust their pay or other payments with the effect of reimbursing them. See David W. Adamany and George E. Agree, *Political Money* (Baltimore: Johns Hopkins University Press, 1975).

[24]Patrick Rivers, *Politics by Pressure* (London: George G. Harrap and Co., 1974), p. 40; Norman Kogan, *The Government of Italy* (New York: Thomas Y. Crowell, 1962), pp. 65–66; and Edwin M. Epstein, *The Corporation in American Politics* (Englewood Cliffs, N.J.: Prentice-Hall, Inc. 1969), pp. 51–53, 90.

[25]"Business Lobbying," *Consumer Reports*, 43 (September 1978), p. 527.

ever, saw an upsurge of public-interest organizations, among them the Nader organizations and the rising consumer movement. In the late seventies, many business people, under attack, stepped up their electoral activity. Looking at the consumer and public-interest organizations of the early seventies, one would see business control of government as declining. Looking at the business backlash that began in the late seventies, one would see it as rising.

The precise extent of business control appears to wax and wane. Over the long run, government regulation of business appears to grow. But so also do new supports or indulgences for business. Along with new restrictions, the U.S. government administers many new financial supports to businesses through tax concessions, loan guarantees, and many other subsidies. These marginal movements do not, in any case, affect the main line of analysis of this chapter. In market systems, since business performs only when induced to do so, government must follow policies that provide the necessary inducements. If from year to year or decade to decade, the pattern of inducement alters, the basic necessity remains.

CHAPTER TEN

INTEREST-GROUP ROLES IN POLICY MAKING

To business managers, interest-group activity counts as only one electoral activity that supplements the controls over government they gain through their privileged position. Many other segments of the citizenry pursue interest-group activity as their principal method of influence on policy, even if they cannot do so with the advantages that business people enjoy.

The play of power engages private interest groups of extraordinary variety—like the National Rifle Association, Air Force Association, American Medical Association, American Postal Workers Union, Farm Bureau Federation, Latex Foam Rubber Council, American Jewish Congress, Paper Bag Institute, Fergus Falls Chamber of Commerce, Florida Dairy Products Association, Clamshell Alliance, and Church League of America, among many thousands of similar national, international, regional, state, and local and neighborhood organizations. Everyone knows a great deal about such interest groups and how they work.

THE GROUP THEORY OF POLITICS

In the pursuit of something profound to say about groups like these, academic political science borrowed from social psychology the once fresh insight that group life molds every human being. From participation in such varied groups as family, play group, classroom, local community, occupational and recreational groups, and larger groups like the town and nation-state, each person learns a variety of skills and attitudes, as well as a respect for rules, that make him or her a functioning participant in that great abstract entity called society. Many political scientists thought that political life too must then be a product of group participation, an idea that gave new prominence to interest groups. "The group basis of politics" became a common term in political science.[1] Political science was probably enriched by the attention it consequently gave to the impact of group life on political attitudes and behavior, even if the ideas were in some measure revivals of insights in, among other places, Plato's *Republic*, Hobbes's *Leviathan*, and Madison's concern over "factions" in Number 10 of *The Federalist Papers*.

But interest groups like those listed do not necessarily, or even most frequently, perform the kind of fundamental functions that form the human being, as in group theory. Participation in an interest group usually amounts to a superficial experience compared to membership in an ethnic group, a family, or a religious sect. Group theory turns out not to tell us much about interest groups.

Perhaps we can at least draw on group theory to ask whether a few fundamental group experiences occur in interest groups—for example, common attitudes come to be shared because of participation or because members form attachments to each other. Not necessarily. Group experience, even of that limited kind, may be absent. Some interest "groups," for example, are hierarchically organized bureaucracies run from the top by one or a few officers. Moreover, the largest single major category of interest group in democratic political systems is, as we have just seen, the business enterprise. Such an enterprise interest "group" may be no group in the ordinary sense but instead a managerial team. Even in a large corporation, a small number of executives wholly determines its interest-group activities. The group experiences of employees or stockholders remain irrelevant to its political activities. The word "group" does not adequately encompass all the kinds of participant in policy making whom we want to analyze.

Indeed the term "interest group" is not at all precise. Some of the participants in policy making who perform what we ordinarily call interest-group activity are individuals, not groups at all. Equivalent in their activities to interest groups, we can identify private individuals of great wealth or other source of influence on policy making: for example, Bernard Baruch, Howard Hughes, David Rockefeller, or Albert Einstein. They operate like interest groups, using their funds and their voices to pull policy in directions they desire; and their influence raises the same questions as the activities of many of the organized groups do.

The study of interest groups now also identifies government officials, their associations, and their departments or agencies as playing

[1]As in Earl Latham, *The Group Basis of Politics* (Ithaca, N.Y.: Cornell University Press, 1952).

interest-group roles. The Joint Chiefs of Staff play an interest-group role in influencing Congress. Reciprocally, individual members of Congress and Congressional committees try to influence the Department of Defense—say, to induce it to locate a military installation in a committee member's congressional district. When public officials play interest-group roles, they do so largely because of the positions into which the rules of government, especially the distribution of authority, have placed them. Not a sociopsychological group feeling but the design of government explains, for example, the interest-group activity of officials of the four states joined in the Colorado River Basin Association or of officials of the Agency for International Development.

To refer to government officials as members of interest groups meets with some resistance. If we set terminological dispute aside, the point worth making is that much official policy-influencing activity is often much like that of private interest groups. If a member of Congress casts a vote in the House, we do not customarily say he or she engaged in interest-group activity. If he telephones an administrator to influence policy, we might say he does so. If joined with a lobbyist in a persuasive luncheon attempt to influence another member of Congress, clearly he does so.

Insofar as a policy maker influences policy through direct exercise of the authority distinctive to that position—congressional votes, presidential vetos, administrative orders—we do not usually label him or her as engaged in interest-group activity. When the policy maker also engages in policy-influencing activities like those practiced by persons without authority, he or she too might be described as playing an interest-group role. The boundary line is vague, however. If an administrator sits and speaks side by side with a lobbyist when testifying before a congressional committee, we might not say he or she engaged in interest-group activity, because it is his or her job to testify for the agency before Congress. On the other hand, we might say that he or she does engage in it, since that activity is indistinguishable from that of the lobbyist beside him.[2]

Very loosely however, we mean by interest-group activities all interactions through which individuals and private groups not holding government authority seek to influence policy, together with those policy-influencing interactions of government officials that go well beyond the direct use of their authority. Engaging in these activities, private groups, individuals, and government groups play indispensable roles in

[2]On presidential "interest-group" activities, see John F. Manley, "Presidential Power and White House Lobbying," *Political Science Quarterly*, 93 (Summer 1978).

policy making. They also make trouble.[3] Let us look into both allegations.

INDISPENSABILITY OF INTEREST-GROUP ACTIVITY

Perhaps the most familiar proposition on the indispensability of these activities declares that they themselves constitute an exercise of free thought, speech, petition, and assembly; hence the exercise of those liberties for which liberal democracy was established. The right of assembly implies the right to organize groups, and in any case the right of free speech requires rights to organize groups and funds to buy newspaper space and broadcast time.

If, on these grounds, we judge the right to organize and/or pursue interest-group activities as indispensable to liberty, the activities are also indispensable in other ways: they perform specific policy-making functions.

Clarifying and Articulating What Citizens Want

A plurality of interest groups are necessary to bring information and analysis to policy problems. We need only call up from earlier chapters the need for information and analysis: inevitable limits on dispassionate nonpartisan analysis, and the consequent dependence of citizens on partisan analysis to help them better understand, reconsider, and press their interests on policy makers. Private interest groups with many members drawn from the citizenry create an informative interchange between the ordinary member and the more informed group leaders. When competition among interest-group leaders for membership ventilates their differences of opinion, the competition educates ordinary citizens who care to attend to the controversies. It also helps them decide which leaders can best serve their interests and deserve their support.

Forming a Feasible Agenda

A technical argument supports such a conclusion. The number of alternative policies that a government might pursue on any issue is at least as large as the number of citizens, each of whom might have his or her own idea of a good policy. No one can debate or vote on all of the thousands or millions of policy alternatives. Somehow the number of alternatives under consideration must be reduced to a manageable few. If policies are to respond at all efficiently to popular will, some persons, through parti-

---

[3]Much of the recent literature on interest groups pursues conceptual precision and empirical verification at the price, I suggest, of consequentiality for such propositions as these two and, though not without merit, is perhaps less useful than older studies are. See, for example, Graham Wooton, *Interest Groups* (Englewood Cliffs, N.J.: Prentice-Hall, Inc., 1970); and Harmon Zeigler and Michael Baer, *Lobbying* (Belmont, Ca.: Wadsworth, 1969). Zeigler's earlier *Interest Groups in American Society* (Englewood Cliffs, N.J.: Prentice-Hall, Inc., 1964) is richer.

san analysis, must find common bonds, preferences, volitions, interests, or strategies to bring the thinking of large numbers of people together, to give up their many diversities in favor of a commonality uniting many of them.

Seen this way, interest-group activity does not simply set segmental or particular interests against common interests. Instead, it sets interests common to each of many sections of the society against an impossible diversity and conflict of individual interests. It does not, however, bring all of the members of the political system to one common or shared view.

A Qualification

To describe private interest groups in these ways somewhat overstates their functions. Many people find themselves in interest groups for reasons having little to do with these functions or with policy making. Trade union members, for example, join unions largely for nonpolitical reasons, for higher wages and for job security. Often group services, rather than the desire to influence policy, will draw members to private interest groups.[4] The American Medical Association, for example, helps to protect against malpractice suits.

Insofar as the citizen affiliates with a private interest group because of its policy activity, he or she may turn to it less as a method of influencing policy than as another device for escaping the task of policy making. Not content with simply delegating proximate policy making to officials, he or she wants also to delegate the task of watching and influencing them. The surveillance function of interest groups is, in some eyes, their principal one. They blow the whistle.

A Special Function in Interactive Policy Making

Interest-group activity in the bureaucracy provides an important form of interactive problem solving when analytical problem solving becomes impossible. Analysis, we saw, is often inconclusive, impossible to complete, or for some other reason unacceptable as a means of choosing among competing policies. An interactive policy–making procedure must then replace it, often, in view of the number of interests in conflict, a highly pluralistic interaction. Voting as one form of interaction can handle only a few of the many issues that government must decide. Even a legislature can handle only a few issues in its interactions. A delegation of authority to a department or bureau chief often becomes the most effective way to settle a policy issue. But on many policies citizens and their leaders fear that such an official may respond to too few of the varied interests of a disparate citizenry. Consequently, a variety of devices are

[4]Mancur Olson, *The Logic of Collective Action* (Cambridge, Mass.: Harvard University Press, 1965), especially chapter 6.

established to compel him or her to interact widely with specified other officials and private interest groups before making a choice of policy. The official may be required, for example, to take the problem to an interdepartmental committee. Or his or her superior may require the consent of certain business groups or other private organizations pertinent to the issues. Or informal rules established by custom may require the official to work out a settlement among several clienteles, as when a regulatory commission seeks agreement for its price setting from the regulated industry, its labor unions, possibly a consumer group, and another agency responsible for fiscal or wage policy. In any case, interaction among a variety of interest groups effectively makes the decision that no one official can conclusively analyze or reach exclusively through his or her own authority.

SOURCES OF INTEREST-GROUP INFLUENCE

Interest-group activity undertaken by government officials achieves an influence because officials can employ their authority indirectly in many ways. What we have just said about functions of interest groups throws some light on how private interest groups achieve influence.

Persuasion

As would be expected from the use of partisan analysis by interest groups to clarify and articulate what people want, one of their main influences on government officials is through persuasion. Interest groups sometimes develop great skill in persuasion through partisan analysis. If an aerospace firm wants a new contract, it will often lobby for it not on the ground that it will enlarge its profits but on some related ground that appeals to the officials' known values: for example, more jobs, or protection of industrial capacity for national defense. A ten-year study of foreign-trade policy making found members of Congress heavily dependent on interest groups for analyzing the implications of pro-business policies for their—the legislators'—own values.[5] Another study, of state rather than national politics, also stresses the research and advisory role of interest groups, as in a comment by a state legislator about lobbyists:

> They can study and present the issues concisely—the average legislator has no time or inclination to do it, and wouldn't understand bills or issues without them. A professional lobbyist in ten minutes can explain what it would take a member two hours to wade through just reading bills.[6]

[5]R. A. Bauer, I. de Sola Pool, and L. A. Dexter, *American Business and Public Policy* (New York: Atherton Press, 1963).
[6]J. C. Wahlke, H. Eulau, W. Buchanan, and L. C. Ferguson, *The Legislative System* (New York: John Wiley and Sons, Inc., 1962), p. 338.

Partisan analysis helps explain the extraordinary effectiveness of some interest-group campaigns directed not at legislators or administrators but at the courts. The NAACP (National Association for the Advancement of Colored People), for example, since 1945 has steadily won gains for blacks in policy on housing, voting rights, transportation, education, and criminal justice by requiring the courts to reconsider the judicial doctrines affecting important questions of policy. One might wonder how an interest group could influence the judiciary unless the judges were corrupt. The answer is that the NAACP uses partisan analysis to persuade judges that inconsistencies between established policies and Constitutional rules call for corrective new policy.

Influence by Rule

Another explanation of interest-group influence arises out of the necessity just noted for interactive instead of analytical solutions to policy problems. To some degree, interest-group politics becomes a kind of a game played by rule by interest-group leaders and policy makers. Some political scientists believe that the game takes something of the "form that it would take if there were no elections or no concern about the nature of public opinion." Officials grant participation in policy making to interest-group leaders whom officials perceive as representatives of interests entitled to consideration by rule. To get into the game an organization is required. Beyond that, publicity and other activities of the group may serve only as rituals.[7]

For many decades, black groups were simply excluded from the benefit of such a rule. Even in a period of rising status for women, the rules recognized by some public officials do not require them to attend to women's organizations with the same concern as for men's. Officials also disregard some interest-group leaders through an invocation of a tacit rule that cranks, fools, and troublemakers deserve no attention and then also assigning thoughtful dissidents to the same category.

Delivering the Vote

These two explanations of private interest-group influence on government officials, persuasion and influence by rule, are sometimes argued to be less important than a third: the ability of groups to influence elections, to deliver the vote. Government officials are alleged to fear the adverse votes of members of private interest groups whom they disappoint.

Many political scientists doubt the adequacy of this explanation. As

[7]V. O. Key, Jr., *Public Opinion and American Democracy* (New York: Alfred A. Knopf, Inc., 1961), p. 351.

one put it, if interest groups try to threaten a public official with their claims to control votes, "they are usually pointing an unloaded gun at the legislator," and he knows it.[8] When, as often holds, group affiliations appear as a relatively fixed element in a citizen's disposition to vote one way or the other, an interest-group leader cannot induce a change in members' votes to reward or punish a public official. Moreover, to tie a group to a party requires a cumbersome process of indoctrination, and once done, the interest-group leader often cannot untie it.

For other reasons too, the interest group often finds it difficult to exert influence by delivering the vote. Elected officials can disregard small groups. In large interest groups like trade unions that contain enough voters to count, they often do not vote alike. Some members vote as trade unionists, some as Catholics, some as conservatives, some as liberals, some as farmers, and so on. Moreover, many organizations have to spend as much of their funds and energy in mobilizing their constituents as in influencing public officials. Both members and public officials have to be persuaded.[9] Finally, many interest-group leaders seek a lasting relation of confidence with a policy maker. Consequently, they cannot threaten. Even if a policy maker offends interest-group leaders on a specific policy, they will want to maintain good relations in order to influence him or her in the future.

On the other hand, an increasing number of interest groups that single-mindedly pursue one issue—pro- or anti-gun control, for example —may find it possible to deliver the vote of a single-issue-minded membership when a multi-issue group like Common Cause cannot. The success of the pro-gun lobbies is an example.

Campaign Support

Only one step removed from delivering the vote, another familiar kind of interest-group influence works effectively. Private interest groups and wealthy individuals can finance campaign expenses for candidates. "They mention in their letters they are officers of such and such association," says a congressman. "All they have to say is . . . if I do what they want, they're in a position to get some campaign funds for me."[10] Potential candidates who cannot find an ally in at least one major interest group often cannot, for lack of finance, run successfully. Legislatures fill with members already disposed, without further word from any interest group, to meet the demands of those who helped them win office.

[8]*Ibid,* p. 522.
[9]William J. Keefe and Morris S. Ogul, *The American Legislative Process,* 3rd ed. (Englewood Cliffs, N.J.: Prentice-Hall, Inc., 1973), pp. 349–53.
[10]"Business Lobbying," *Consumer Reports,* 43 (September 1978), p. 530.

Interest-Group Leaders as an Elite

Along with the three elites already identified—knowledgeables, policy makers, and businesspeople—we might designate interest-group leaders as an elite. Interest-group leaders range from persons of great influence to persons merely busy rather than influential. Using the term "elite" as we do to refer to small groups (small relative to the whole citizenry) of greatly disproportionate political control, influence, or power, the most influential interest-group leaders would qualify. Among those qualifying as elite, we mention in particular those to whom policy makers grant actual authority. Governmental policy makers sometimes largely delegate their own authority to private parties, as we have already noted they sometimes do for business managers. Committees of the American Bar Association, not government officials, for example, wrote the corporate laws of at least fifteen states.

TROUBLESOME ASPECTS OF INTEREST GROUPS

Although interest-group activity makes indispensable contributions to policy making, it also makes trouble. Most people know some of the reasons why.

Political Inequality

Interest-group activity is a source of great political inequality that does not square with democratic norms. Inequality among persons is sometimes gilded over by allegations that the many groups in a democratic system exercise a roughly equal influence in politics. If true, the allegation itself would point at another inequality. For if groups differing greatly in size, the mammoth AFL-CIO and the much smaller National Association of Manufacturers, actually exercised roughly equal political influence, that necessarily would mean that each member of the AFL-CIO had far less influence than each member of the smaller organization.

But interest groups do not and cannot exert equal influence. But then, on the other hand, neither does influence correspond with number of members. Business interest groups, we have seen, have the advantage of better organization and finance over other groups. Aside from that major inequality, many others are apparent. Members of the medical profession, for example, draw on advantages of organization and finance for interest-group activity. The rules of the play of power also grant them an unusually large influence on policy making in certain areas. Organizations representing or potentially representing many more citizens, like the Urban League or Common Cause, face harder sledding. Of course, many potential interests never achieve effective organization because their potential members are not well enough off to finance it.

Although the vote is distributed relatively equally, all the other instruments of control available to interest groups—analytical skills, money, and organizational skill and readiness—are distributed most unequally. At an extreme, as already noted, a single wealthy person on his or her own can achieve the same political influence as a poorly financed mass organization. We shall further examine political inequality in a later chapter—in interest-group activities and in its other appearances in the play of power.

Subordination of Common to Segmental Interests

A common allegation complains that interest groups neglect the common welfare in a pursuit of their own narrow or segmental interests. Although a plausible allegation, it calls for caution. Perhaps strictly speaking, interests shared by all do not exist, only a diversity of segmental interests does. Even on an interest in survival—specifically, say, an interest in forestalling nuclear warfare—people's opinions do in fact diverge on the circumstances in which they would want to survive and in the risks they would wish to accept. Politically, they differ, for example, in what risk of nuclear war they would choose to run in negotiation with or ultimatum to the Soviet Union or China, just as they differed over whether President Kennedy should have risked nuclear war in the Cuban missile crisis.

These obvious marginal differences of opinion do not deny, however, such commonalities as a desire to avoid nuclear destruction, to avoid exhaustion of energy resources, to avoid widespread economic depression, to reduce some kinds of crime, to improve education, or to develop methods of conflict reconciliation that avoid civil war. Quite possibly, interest-group activity emphasizes the marginal differences rather than these commonalities.

If so, such an emphasis may make more trouble in the future. In the past, policy making has been occupied mostly with "who gets what" issues: taxation, labor relations, farm policy, and industrial regulations, among others. Although some issues have raised questions about the welfare of all—issues like national defense—policy making seems to have shifted significantly in that direction only in recent years. New common welfare issues have appeared in arms control, energy conservation, environmental protection, population control, and economic growth. If interest-group activity were well suited to the older "who gets what" issues —and the critics doubt even that—it may cope badly with the newer problems on whose solution depends the welfare of all.

Yet segmental interests do in fact exist and present worthy moral and legal claims. A political system that pursued common interests to the exclusion of segmental interests we would consider intolerable. The liberal democratic tradition applauds diversity in interest, opinion, and activity. Moreover, the deprived segments of the population presumably need opportunities to pursue their segmental interests.

Moreover, much interest-group activity pursues not narrow, self-serving segmental interests but visions of a common interest. Opponents of nuclear electric power, energy conservationists, foreign-policy advocates of a tough line toward the Soviet Union, many proponents of reform of public education, and broad purpose organizations like Common Cause or the Nader groups will often claim that they battle for the common interest. As the point was once put, "the members of the American League to Abolish Capital Punishment were not a group of people in danger of being hanged."[11]

The Veto in the Democratic Play of Power

The problem of conflict between broad and narrow interests often traces to the man-made rules of the play of power, specifically rules that disperse the authority to veto or stop a policy. The President can veto anything that Congress initiates. A minority of members can stop either House from acting. Either House in Congress can veto the other simply by inaction. Within each House dozens of committees can stop or delay legislation. The states can stop federal legislation in certain areas. The federal government can call a halt to state action in others.

Outside the complex procedures of government itself, the rules distribute veto authority even more widely. Additional veto authority rests largely on the autonomy of the business enterprise, often neglected in political science. As we have seen, a market system requires that on many points the enterprise be legally protected in its right to say no to the state. The privileged position of business permits it to obstruct policies on environmental pollution and decay, energy shortage, inflation and unemployment, and distribution of income and wealth when such policies might damage business.[12] Labor unions can exercise a highly effective veto on wage controls.

Because veto powers are broadly distributed, interest groups converge on persons who can exercise vetoes. To stop a policy move, they need influence only one of the many persons or bodies that can exercise a veto. To move a policy ahead, they must influence all potential sources of veto. It is little wonder then that interest groups obstruct the new policies that may be required to pursue our common or shared interests.

[11]E. E. Schattschneider, *The Semisovereign People* (New York: Holt, Rinehart, and Winston, Inc., 1960), p. 26.

[12]The preceding two paragraphs have been paraphrased from Charles E. Lindblom, *Politics and Markets* (New York: Basic Books, 1977), pp. 346–47.

Already noted in earlier chapters, a broad distribution of veto powers in democracies reflects their historical concern with personal liberty rather than popular control over policy. Fearful that governments might intervene excessively, the designers of democratic systems permitted many participants, both governmental and private, to stop the initiatives of government officials. This decision may have been wise, but they bought such protection for individual liberty at a high price, a price that may be rising in an era of collective rather than distributional problems. If vetoes can stop policy initiatives at many points, groups of citizens can control their government only when they want it to desist. Neither they nor a majority can control it when they want it to act.

To date, the democratic world has had almost no experience with interest-group activity not tied tightly to broadly distributed veto powers. We can hardly imagine how interest-group activity might operate in other circumstances. Its indispensability to both personal freedom and to producing informed policies might loom much larger, and its drawbacks might diminish. On the other hand, market decision making gives us a different clue. Business enterprises in the market are ordinarily permitted to proceed with their initiatives without a veto from government, from competitors, or from any source. As a result, market systems achieve high rates of change and innovation, together with frequent great injury to other firms, the environment, and to their own customers. Clearly, the right distribution of veto power poses a difficult question.

CHAPTER ELEVEN

POLITICAL INEQUALITY

In the play of power, the list of principal players includes elected and appointed government officials, together with party and interest-group leaders and a small number of highly active citizens. The great mass of citizens actively enter the play infrequently and then only in small roles. They face, we have seen, a variety of obstructions if they wish to exercise control over policy making. Some obstructions reside simply in the complexity of large-scale government: a great multiplicity of participants, and a near bewildering variety of grants of authority. Some reside in procedures ostensibly designed for liberty rather than popular control: separation of powers, checks and balances, and two-thirds rather than simple-majority rules in legislative voting on some issues. Citizen control is also often obstructed, we saw, by bureaucratic politics and by legislative procedures designed to suit the convenience of legislators rather than to hold them responsive to the citizens' wishes on policy. The many unpredictabilities of mutual adjustment among officials and party and interest-group leaders are another obstacle. So is the easy efficacy of vetoes that can be cast by many participants at many points in the policy-making process. No less important than any of these obstacles, the privileged position of business people and their advantages in interest-group activity combine to reduce citizen control even further.

Perhaps we should list as another obstacle the unpredictable outcomes of attempts to make citizen control over policy making more effective. We have seen that all rules for the play of power and all allocations of authority produce unpredictable indirect uses of authority. Reforms in the rules or in the authority structure constantly misfire to a significant degree, for example, as did attempts to reform the presidential nominating process. A kind of residual uncontrollability of the play of power consequently stands squarely in the way of citizen control over policy making.

Political inequality among citizens is another major obstruction to citizen control over policy making.

THE DUBIOUS NORM OF POLITICAL INEQUALITY

Strictly speaking, political inequality does not deprive citizens of control; it simply implies that some citizens exercise more control than others do. The norm of political equality harks back to the axiom that democracy requires not simply control by citizens but an equal distribution among them of rights of or capacities for control. As a norm, most people give it rhetorical support; and its influence pervades society, especially in America, as de Tocqueville in the 1830s and others since him have observed.

The norm does not command universal support. Aside from self-serving desires of favored groups to protect their inegalitarian advantages, as in white-black relations or relations between wealthy and poor, people oppose political equality on other grounds. Neither political equality nor popular control may be highly valued by persons who want policy making to become more informed and more carefully analyzed. Instead, they may want policy-making responsibility to be given to competent people. They may want the better informed and educated citizens to exercise disproportionately great influence on policy making. Most people want most decisions to be parceled out to competent decision makers: most decisions on technology to scientists and engineers, on medical care to the medical profession, on monetary policy to bankers and economists, and so on. If they want political equality at all, they want it only to control some decisions, such as those on who shall hold office.

Some people care greatly neither about equality nor inequality. They judge other considerations as more relevant to policy making. Some want policy making to be highly adaptable, capable of innovation. In reverse, some want it to maintain stability or continuity. Some people believe that the main problem of any society is simply to keep the social peace, and they ask only that policy making not rock the boat. Some people have in their minds a vision of an ideal society in the light of which they believe that the best policy-making system is the one that will bring society closer to that ideal. At an extreme, they may believe that they know which policies are correct and incorrect, in which case they may opt for the policy-making system which they think most likely to reach correct policies. Taking quite a different tack, out of concern for human fallibility, some people may opt for a system that responds to the widest possible range of opinions and interests, one permeated by challenge, counter-challenge, and one that reaches only interim policy decisions in a never-ending revision of policy. All such people may set equality and inequality aside as unimportant.

Egalitarians themselves differ on the meaning of political equality. Does political equality call in principle for the equal influence of all citizens on each piece of legislation? Or on the package of policies that a party might present to the voters? Or simply on choice of representatives who, after their election, can freely legislate as they think best? Does equality in principle call merely for equality in the vote, for equality in participation in interest groups, or for equality in other forms of influence as well?

Acknowledging that political equality does not stand as a generally accepted nor as a well defined criterion for policy making, we nevertheless propose to examine political inequality as it influences a citizen's capacity to control policy making. Kinds and degrees of political inequality are illuminating, even if the implications drawn from them will differ from person to person.

BASIC INEQUALITIES

Legally imposed inequalities aside, many citizens find little motivation to participate actively in policy. Fully one-third of American citizens neither votes, joins interest groups, does party work, communicates with their representatives, nor discusses politics with their friends (except occasionally in a vague and uninformed way). The following table shows the pattern. Apparently by their own free choice, millions of citizens effectively grant to others much greater influence than they keep for themselves.

Approximate Percentage of American Citizens Participating in Various Forms of Political Activity

	Percent
Report regularly voting in Presidential elections	72
Report always voting in local elections	47
Active in at least one organization in community problems	32
Have worked with others in trying to solve some community problems	30
Have very actively worked for a party or candidate during an election	26
Have ever contacted a local government official about some issue or problem	20
Have attended at least one political meeting or rally in last three years	19
Have ever formed a group or organization to attempt to solve some local community problem	14
Have ever given money to a party or candidate during an election campaign	13
Presently a member of a political club or organization	8
Have ever attempted to persuade others to vote as they were	28
Have ever contacted a state or national government official about some issue or problem	18

From Sidney Verba and Norman H. Nie, *Participation in America* (New York: Harper & Row, Publishers, 1972) p. 31.

Despite their inactivity, do the inactive always have an opportunity to participate in choosing and influencing officials if they wish? Legally, they do. Yet disproportionately those who participate less have less income and less status.[1] The correlation among participation and income and status is fundamental. Perhaps then the difference between the more and the less active participants is not simply in their free and happy choices to participate or not, but in other inequalities related to income and status.

Information, Analysis, and Education

One inequality among citizens appears in their information on issues and about the play of power. Studies of presidential-election years find sharp differences in the extent to which citizens seek political information.

The percentage of American citizens (in the samples studied) engaging or not engaging in various information-acquiring activities are as follows (for a period of four presidential elections):

	Percent
Read newspaper articles about the election	70–80
Do not	30–20
Read about campaign in magazines	30–40
Do not	70–60
Watched programs about campaign on television	50–90
Do not	50–10

From University of Michigan Survey Research Center as quoted in Robert H. Salisbury, *Governing America* (New York: Appleton Century–Crofts, 1973) p. 57.[2]

Why these inequalities in information and in disposition to seek it? Among other causes, people differ in their capacity to understand and use information both about issues and about the play of power. A University of Michigan Survey Research Center study of the level of information and understanding of voters ascertained how voters formulated issues:

For:

15½ percent of voters, the vote was related to an organized set of ideas
45 percent, the vote was related to group benefits
23 percent, the vote was related vaguely to the nature of the times
17½ percent, the vote seemed unrelated to any public issue.

A. Campbell, P. E. Converse, W. E. Miller, and D. E. Stokes, *The American Voter* (New York: John Wiley and Sons, Inc., 1960) p. 249.

[1]Sidney Verba and Norman H. Nie, *Participation in America* (New York: Harper & Row, Publishers, 1972), p. 338.
[2]Later studies show a rise in voter ability to conceptualize. But the inequality continues: N. H. Nie, S. Verba, and J. R. Petrocik, *The Changing American Voter* (Cambridge, Mass.: Harvard University Press, 1976), chapter 7.

Educational inequality helps explain these differences. High rates of political participation correlate with high familiarity with issues. Both correlate with education: the more educated participate most heavily.[3] Only half of those who have not graduated from high school, but four-fifths of the college educated, play active roles in organizations.[4] Political issues, as well as the design of strategies to gain personal influence in the play of power, are hopelessly beyond the competence of the poorly educated citizen.

Socialization

In large part, people participate in the play of power because taught, indoctrinated, or socialized to do so. They learn from family, school, friends, clubs, and political parties the attitudes and dispositions to action which lead them to vote and otherwise participate.[5] People participate only if they have been taught to believe it matters, if taught the skills of citizenship, if indoctrinated with aspirations and expectations that stimulate rather than paralyze, and if taught to see themselves as members of the political community. A citizen not socialized in any of these ways will not vote or otherwise participate in policy making. Even if he knows which policies would help him and even if this citizen would like to do something positive about his problems, he will not see in voting or other participation any practical, realizable possibility of helping himself (and incidentally, this view may be as rational as that of the activist citizen).

The patterns or failures of socialization of millions of nineteenth-century immigrants to the United States crippled them politically, either temporarily or for their lifetimes in America. Today the largest inactive group is the disadvantaged blacks and other poor, uneducated minorities cut off from socializing groups and without habits, aspirations, or expectations supporting participation.[6] Their social isolation from politically active people impedes their acquiring the most elementary necessary political information and skill.

A more massive failure of socialization toward political participation is positive socialization against it, that is, toward withdrawal or nonparticipation. Many investigators have found evidence that public schools discourage participation through their emphasis on submission to au-

---

[3]Sidney Verba and Norman H. Nie, *Participation in America* (New York: Harper & Row, Publishers, 1972), p. 263.

[4]*Ibid*, p. 181.

[5]*Ibid*, pp. 19, 133, and *passim.*

[6]Perhaps a million and a half are simply not allowed to vote. Even if the law says they can, informal, extralegal rules are enforced to prohibit them from doing so.

thority. Moreover, the schools appear to do so more for working-class children than upper-class children.[7]

Inequalities of information, education, and socialization converge. People differ greatly in their personal capacities to understand the play of power, in their belief that they can influence it, and in their effectiveness in it. For political influence in the play of power, they need time, knowledge of public affairs, skill in partisan analysis, a persuasive tongue or pen, status in the community, influential associates, and success in interpersonal relations. Millions of citizens lack these skills, and only a few possess all of them. One can contrast New York City's Puerto Ricans with a graduating class at Harvard or Stanford.

Political Organizations

Beyond voting and using one's persuasive efforts on friends and neighbors, if one has the information and talent to do so, participation in choosing and influencing public officials requires an organization. Alone, the ordinary citizen can do almost nothing. He or she has to work through interest groups or campaign organizations by giving them time, skill, or money.

The words "skill" and "money" reveal the inequalities. Because many citizens have no skills to offer to an interest group, they can in no way become an influence in it or through it. They do not know how to play a useful organizational role, hardly dare to try, and are indifferently regarded by the actives in organizations. Other citizens can practice any of a variety of organizational skills. They can persuade, negotiate, analyze issues, or write position papers. The highly educated, for example, find it easy to play some significant role in political organizations and are usually warmly welcomed to active membership. They stand in sharp contrast to their more numerous fellow citizens.

There also are great inequalities in money and political organizations. Some individuals in the United States can and do contribute to political organizations more than the entire income of many less affluent citizens. At an extreme, when Nelson Rockefeller contributed one million dollars toward his own campaign expenses, he threw into the play of power a sum that would be difficult to raise from even as many as a hundred thousand persons of average to low income. Organizations need to pay newspapers, broadcasting stations, and their own office staffs, and to engage speech writers, television producers, "advance men," lobbyists, publicists, and a long list of others. They also need money for typewriters, copying machines, postage, telephones—all the elementary

---

[7]Robert D. Hess and Judith V. Torney, *The Development of Political Attitudes in Children* (Chicago: Aldine 1967). See also Samuel Bowles and Herbert Gintis, *Schooling in Capitalist America* (New York: Basic Books, 1976).

tools of politics.[8] Despite their great numbers, the poor can afford only poor political organizations, and the well-off finance a variety of better ones. Not simply an inequality between the very affluent and the poor, inequality in organizations runs through the whole society. Union members, among the better paid American workers, mobilize far less money for political organizations than do businesspeople.[9]

Wealth, Favors, and Deference

What we have said about money in organizations understates its importance as a source of inequality in democratic policy making. The influence of wealth runs through many channels. One goes through financing persuasion, as in contributions to campaign expenses. A congressman says, "We deal in two things here—votes and the money used to persuade votes."[10] Another channel goes through the buying of political favors and thus directly exerting control. The line between the two channels blurs, for example, when a donor disguises a bribe as a contribution to a candidate's television expenses. Many people know that there is an old tradition in American politics that a large enough contribution can buy an ambassadorial appointment. Less conspicuously and with an unknown frequency, contributions and other favors can buy desired legislative votes or administrative rulings. Often entirely within the law, money cements the loyalties of political affiliates in parties and interest groups.

Because wealthy people can reward other people, many habitually defer to them and confer authority on them. Some people simply accept leadership from the wealthy, and many people allow themselves to be influenced by the prospect of favors that the wealthy can offer to those about them. Some legislators, for example, find it difficult to refuse free airplane trips, the loan of automobiles, and the pleasures of dinner parties and weekends with the wealthy. Even if under these circumstances the legal and informal rules of American politics succeed in prohibiting an explicit exchange of favor for favor, a policy maker nevertheless will feel a more solicitous concern for the wealthy than if he had not come to regard them as friends.

Among those of greatest wealth, disproportionate participation in the play of power warrants considering them to be an elite, the last elite we shall introduce into the analysis. We first introduced an elite of knowledge with powers of persuasion, then a governmental policy-making elite

---

[8]See A. Heard, *The Costs of Democracy* (Chapel Hill: University of North Carolina Press, 1960); A. Heard, *Money and Politics* (New York: Public Affairs Committee, Inc., 1956); and Herbert E. Alexander, ed., *Campaign Money* (New York: The Free Press, 1976).

[9]Charles E. Lindblom, *Politics and Markets* (New York: Basic Books, 1977), pp. 194–99.

[10]"Business Lobbying," *Consumer Reports*, 43 (September 1978), p. 529.

with authority, then a business elite with a privileged position resting largely on political exchange, and then an interest-group elite employing various sources of influence. In an industrialized society in which great wealth is based on industry rather than on land, the elite of wealth tends to merge with the elite of business, both taking their advantage in the play of power from what they can offer in exchange to induce people to do as they wish.

PART THREE

THE CITIZEN IN THE PLAY OF POWER

CHAPTER TWELVE

THE IMPRECISION OF VOTING

Despite all the forms of political inequality, at least the vote is equally distributed in democratic systems. No, it is not. Until 1920, women in the United States could not vote in some states nor in federal elections, and legal restrictions on black voting have eroded only slowly. In metropolitan areas, boundary lines separating local governments both give and take away voting rights. The New Jersey resident who works every day in Manhattan cannot vote there. The few hundred thousand citizens of Wyoming elect the same number of senators as do the millions of residents of the state of New York. In state senates too, some legislators represent a multiple of the number of citizens represented by other representatives. The "size" of a citizen's vote, consequently, depends on where he or she lives. Rules that require two-thirds rather than simple majorities—in legislatures, referenda, or for amendments to the Constitution—again give some citizens or their representatives twice the voting power of others, since one vote against something cancels two votes for it.

Inequalities in voting aside, voting is on several counts a weak instrument of policy making. A now common argument that can be traced to Joseph Schumpeter's competitive theory of democracy ("competitive" because voters simply choose among competing, would-be rulers)[1] alleges that the vote typically permits citizens to decide who will make policy but does not give them a significant influence over policy. In fact, voters usually do vote for candidates rather than for policies (although occasionally they vote directly on a few policy issues). It does not follow, however, that the voters necessarily surrender all significant influence on

[1]Joseph Schumpeter, *Capitalism, Socialism, and Democracy,* 3rd ed. (New York: Harper & Row, Publishers, 1949), chapter 22.

policy. Candidates to some degree tailor their policy commitments to suit voters. They know that re-election may depend on which policies they have inaugurated or failed to inaugurate. Citizens also influence policy through interest-group activity. Just how weak a control over policy the vote gives the ordinary citizen remains an open question that we shall now explore further.

LOOSENESS OF VOTER CONTROL

A Gallup poll on fourteen policy issues shows government policy coinciding with or disagreeing with public opinion as follows:

Policy	Majority Opinion Congruent with Existing Policy?
Decreased defense spending	No
Wage and price controls	No
Busing schoolchildren for racial integration	No
Gun registration	No
Aid to parochial schools	No
Establishment of diplomatic relations with Cuba	No
Unconditional amnesty	Yes
Legalization of marihuana	Yes
Equal Rights Amendment	Yes
Federal financing of congressional elections	No
Death penalty	No
5 percent income surtax	Yes
Decreased spending for social programs	Yes
Legalized abortions	Yes

George C. Edward III and Ira Sharkansky, *The Policy Predicament* (San Francisco: W. H. Freeman and Co., 1978), p. 20.

According to the poll, policy conformed to public opinion on six issues; on nine it did not. We already have found many reasons why policy does not conform more often than that. What additional inadequacies in citizen control over policy arise out of the voting process?

Voter Ignorance

Voting for members of Congress and lesser officials proceeds under circumstances in which the typical voter knows little about the names, backgrounds, experience, and reputations of the candidates; less about what policies each stands for; and still less about whether they can or will do anything to implement their espoused policies. Studies indicate that most people do not know their representatives' names. Nor can many identify their positions on conspicuous public issues. Not knowing a candidate's position on issues, they often choose on other grounds, such as personality or party affiliation.[2]

[2]Several studies are summarized in George C. Edward III and Ira Sharkansky, *The Policy Predicament* (San Francisco: W. H. Freeman and Co., 1978), pp. 23–27.

Issues Not Put to Voters

Moreover, candidates do not take a stand on most policy issues at elections. Most issues come up only after an election, are acted on as they arise, and die before the next election. Between elections, legislators and administrative policy makers settle, for example, most foreign policy decisions, many changes in tax and monetary policy, and decisions on space exploration. Because each Congress acts on thousands of bills, clearly it will not ventilate many of its issues for voters at election time. Inescapably on most policy questions citizens must abdicate.[3]

Single Dimension of the Vote

A vote for a new policy or for a candidate who advocates it might be regarded also as implying a vote as well for new taxes to cover its costs. Presumably, in order to use the vote as an effective instrument, a voter needs to be able to vote yes or no depending on what new taxes will be imposed. Voting ordinarily offers few possibilities of knowing this and voting accordingly. The decision on raising the money for the new program will be made at another time, often by other people.

To use the vote effectively, a voter also needs to know whether the inauguration of the new program which a candidate recommends implies the termination of some old program. In other words, the voter always needs to know, before voting, the implication of choice for other choices. For example, before voting for an opponent of nuclear power, the voter needs to know what alternative power sources will be developed if nuclear power is abandoned. Or he or she may want to vote for nuclear power if safety standards are meticuously enforced, but against it if they are not. Voting almost always proceeds without specifying essential conditions or implications like these. A ballot consequently does not permit the voter to express anything but the crudest of choices with a high probability that these wishes will be misread.

The Problem of the One Vote Versus Many Policies

For the informed voter who knows precisely what he or she wants and what the candidates stand for, there remains another obstacle to making that vote effective. Each voter has one vote but many policy preferences. If he or she agrees with candidate Smith on fifteen issues out of the twenty-five on which Smith has declared a position, but agrees with candidate McNally on the remaining ten, how can a single vote for Smith tell Smith on which issues the voter agrees? A voter may even vote for McNally even though agreeing with Smith on most issues, if McNally's few seem more important; but, again, that vote fails to communicate

---

[3]We earlier saw that individual members of the Congress often abdicate in large part to legislative leaders, especially to the members of the various policy committees and to their chairs. The double abdication leaves only loose ties between votes and policy.

anything to the winning candidate about what he or she wishes on each of the issues.[4]

Paradoxes and Other Problems

In multiparty systems like those in Western Europe, voters sometimes vote for a panel of candidates in systems of proportional representation. In the United States, ordinarily, voters choose among candidates to fill a single office. Each of many possible systems of voting and of counting votes differs in the way it selects candidates in response to the voters' expressed wishes. The superiority of one system over another depends on the kinds of issues, the cleavages among voters, the intensity of their preference for one policy over another or one candidate over another, and other factors.[5] These factors shift constantly, with the result that, even if a voting system produces good results in one election, it may serve voters poorly in another election. Clearly, in all voting, even in a show of hands in a committee meeting, voting will serve well or badly depending upon how, in the light of the pattern of opinion among members of the group, the issues are posed. A vote may misrepresent opinion either because of how alternatives are formulated or because of the order in which they were put to a vote.

A fundamental difficulty of extraordinary logical complexity arises from difficulties in inferring a social preference—what society should do —from individual preference. When all or a large majority of voters prefer A over B, and an election shows A winning over B, most people would say that the election results make sense. But if only fifty-one percent of the voters prefer A to B but none intensely so, and forty-nine percent of the voters intensely prefer B to A, we feel less sure that A's winning makes sense.

A well-known paradox illustrates the problem of determining social preference in greater depth. Suppose there are three alternative policies or candidates and a three-way division of opinion among voters. One-third of the voters prefers alternative A to B, B to C, and consistently then, A to C. Another third prefers B to C, C to A and again consistently, B to A. A final third prefers C to A, A to B and consistently, C to B. It follows, then, that a majority favors A over B. A majority also favors B over C. But a majority also favors C over A. Each alternative shows a

---

[4]The frequent claim by the winning candidate that he or she has a mandate from the electorate to lower taxes, to take a harder line with the Soviet Union, or to cut federal payrolls is ordinarily fraudulent. Ordinarily the candidate does not know whether he or she won the election because of or in spite of a stand on any single issue. If the candidate does know that he or she won on some single issue, then it will follow that on all other issues he or she has no mandate and is without any adequate expression of the voters' wishes on any of them.

[5]See Douglas Rae, *The Political Consequences of Electoral Laws* (New Haven, Conn.: Yale University Press, 1967).

majority over each of the other two. Counting preferences does not give us an unambiguous statement of society's preference.[6] No voting system can solve such problems as these.

HELP FROM POLITICAL PARTIES?

In their competition with each other, political parties help a voter reduce some of the obstacles to an effective use of the vote. Party competition gives a voter only modest, limited influence on policy, to be sure, but larger than might be expected. Parties formulate a package of mutually supportive policy proposals to which candidates of the party are to some degree tied. A voter can then weigh and choose among two or a few parties more easily than among dozens of candidates for various offices, each with his or her own program.

In the British system, national party officials exert great control over the selection of candidates and frequently refuse to give party standing to elected officials who no longer remain loyal to party directives. Consequently, the parties tie candidates to their party's platform, so that the voter can predict, if he takes the trouble to familiarize himself with the party's general position, what many of its specific policies are likely to be. The voter then needs to know nothing about candidates other than their party affiliation.[7]

In the American system, party, candidates, and policy are only loosely tied together. Parties commit themselves only vaguely on policy, and candidates often freely disavow the party platform.[8] But the tie does not wholly dissolve. (In some American states, party discipline actually holds legislators to a position as firmly as it does in some of the European democracies.) Up through the 1950s and into the sixties, studies confirmed what common experience suggested: that the parties had a general position from which the voter could infer its general policy position. In one study, questionnaires returned by party leaders showed, not surprisingly, that Democratic leaders

> typically display the stronger urge to elevate the lowborn, the uneducated, the deprived minorities, and the poor in general. . . . They are more critical of wealth and big business and more eager to bring them under regula-

[6]See Kenneth Arrow, *Social Choice and Individual Values* (New York: John Wiley and Sons, Inc. 1951) for additional difficulties in inferring social from individual preferences.

[7]For more on British parties, see R. T. McKenzie, *British Political Parties* (New York: Frederick A. Praeger, 1964).

[8]On the degree to which voters see issues as interrelated in some way, so that party packages of issues can be made somewhat coherent, see Warren E. Miller and Teresa E. Levitan, *Leadership and Change* (Cambridge, Mass.: Winthrop Publishers, 1976).

tion. . . . The Republican leaders subscribe in greater measure to the symbols and practices of individualism, *laissez faire,* and national independence.[9]

Even then, some Republicans in Congress were and are in these respects more Democratic than most Democrats, and some Democrats more Republican than most Republicans, as in the long-standing conservative coalition in Congress.[10] The guideline to voting offered by party identification sometimes misleads the voter.

In the 1970s, party commitment to issues declined, and parties were less helpful in offering the voter a coherent pattern simplifying the difficulties of voting. The Democratic party extended its appeals to almost all groups in the population, including even the high-income and business groups. The Republican party might be described as having moved somewhat from a recognizable ideological position to a reactive stance, its leaders, especially state and local, simply objecting to many of the strongest currents of contemporary thought and politics. Under these circumstances, Democratic party candidates may stand for any of a number of possible conflicting positions, and the voter can infer little from the candidate's party label. Republican candidates often appeal to voters despite rather than because of party label.[11]

Do voters in fact usually vote on party lines rather than on an independent appraisal of candidates? From decade to decade, party loyalty varies. In recent years, about forty percent of the American population has voted independently of party; other voters are strongly or weakly partisan.[12]

Parties and Agreed Policies

Party competition helps the voter in another way too—by drawing all candidates toward policy on which the majority of voters clearly agree. When parties must compete to win elections, party leadership must seek

[9]H. McClosky, P. J. Hoffman, and R. O'Hara, "Issue Conflict and Consequences Among Party Leaders and Followers," *American Political Science Review,* 54 (June 1960).

[10]John F. Manley, "The Conservative Coalition in Congress," *American Behavioral Scientist,* 17 (November–December 1973).

[11]Everett C. Ladd, Jr. and Charles D. Hadley, *Transformations of the American Party System* (New York: W. W. Norton & Co., Inc., 1975), chapter 6.

[12]Norman H. Nie, Sidney Verba, and John R. Petrocik, *The Changing American Voter* (Cambridge, Mass.: Harvard University Press, 1976), p. 49. From decade to decade or even from election to election, voters' concern with issues, attachment to party, and patterns of agreement with other voters shifts. We are not concerned here with the movements but instead are trying to capture the main mechanism pertinent to citizen control of policy making. On important changes in electoral behavior and in voters' relations with candidates, issues, and parties, see also Everett C. Ladd, Jr. and Charles D. Hadley, *Transformations of the American Party System* (New York: W. W. Norton & Co., Inc., 1975) and Warren E. Miller and Teresa E. Levitan, *Leadership and Change* (Cambridge, Mass.: Winthrop Publishers, 1976).

out information on citizen preferences beyond the inadequate information revealed to the party by election results. Parties then will tend to offer voters all policies preferred by a clear large majority of citizens: for example, preservation of law and order, honesty in government, high-level employment, and reasonable price stability. For the full import of this conclusion, imagine two parties competing to win an election. At the last moment the election is canceled and a winning party chosen by a toss of a coin. If both parties had offered voters those policies wanted by a clear large majority, on those issues it would not matter to voters which party won the toss. The effect of the anticipated election would have been to drive both parties to nearly identical positions on each of the policies favored by an unmistakable majority.

Limits on Party Effectiveness

Parties often fail to help voters use their votes effectively in the ways described for several reasons.

Minorities' Control of Policy. Parties sometimes help minorities rather than majorities. Sometimes a party captures voters by adopting for each policy a position appealing to a minority with intense preferences who will come to the polls rather than appealing on each issue to a more apathetic majority. A party or candidates may put together a winning coalition of voters by appealing to "gun lovers" by promising to vote against gun controls, to business with promises of low taxes, to Russophobes with a pledge of a tough foreign policy, and so on. They win, but not by serving as an instrument of the majorities.[13]

Voters Drawn to Party other than by its Policies. Nor can parties perform as described if voters follow them regardless of policy issues. Voters often do not support a party because of its stand but simply because they were born into it. For the 1960s, for example, one study showed that among adults, seventy to eighty percent of the offspring of active party members (when both parents belonged to the same party) identified themselves as members of their parents' party, as did sixty to seventy percent of the offspring of inactive party members.[14] Although most American voters used to form their party loyalties while still in grade school, by the 1970s new voters were less inclined to follow their parents' party choice than in the fifties.[15] When parental influence is not important, the new voter

---

[13]An illuminating theoretical discussion of this possibility and of its implications for democratic theory is in R. A. Dahl, *A Preface to Democratic Theory* (Chicago: University of Chicago Press, 1956), chapters 4 and 5.

[14]A. Campbell, P. E. Converse, W. E. Miller, and D. E. Stokes, *The American Voter* (New York: John Wiley and Sons, Inc., 1960), p. 147.

[15]Norman H. Nie, Sidney Verba, and John R. Petrocik, *The Changing American Voter* (Cambridge, Mass.: Harvard University Press, 1976), pp. 350–52.

may see himself or herself as an independent. Or a new attachment to party may be acquired without regard to party policies, from the groups with which the voter associates or to which he or she refers for political orientation: church, union, ethnic group, intellectual milieu, occupational group, or social class, for example. Parties often discourage voters from attaching to party on policy grounds. They deliberately try to attract voters with slogans, general and abstract declarations, colorful candidates, and pageantry, while avoiding a commitment on policy.

Parties That Do Not Try to Win.   The argument that party competition gives citizens an influence in the play of power in policy making, both generally and on specific issues, rests, of course, on the assumption that parties compete to win. Party pursuit of other objectives sometimes takes priority over winning, especially when the party's ideology constrains it. For various reasons a party may fail to compete wholeheartedly. It was widely believed, for example, that many local and state lower- and middle-level Republican party leaders supported Senator Barry Goldwater for the presidential nomination in 1964 because his candidacy would strengthen their power in the party relative to the central national leadership of the party and not because they thought he could win.

Lack of Party Solidarity.   Party competition on policy can give the voter control over policy to the extent that candidates follow the party position once elected. As we have noted, candidates do so in many European democracies and in some American states, but less so in most American states and in American national politics.[16] We already have noted that in recent years, either as a passing phase or as a long-term trend, party solidarity has declined, especially in the Democratic party as it reaches out to include almost every element in society. It is increasingly difficult to characterize the distinctive policy tendencies of either American party; hence increasingly difficult for a voter to know what policies are likely to become less or more probable as a result of the victory of one party or the other.

[16]Many Americans live in municipalities in which party competition is ineffective, and many live in states in which competition within a party has to replace, if anything does, competition between parties. In these circumstances, factions within the parties take on some of the characteristics of parties, and just as there are two-party and multiparty regimes, so there also are bifactional and multifactional regimes.

Factional rivalry does not play quite the same role in policy making as does party rivalry. Factions lack continuity both in name and in actual structure. Hence the voter does not necessarily know to which faction a candidate belongs, nor if he knows at one date does he necessarily know at a later date. Effective competition between the factions is weakened by the ease with which members can change from one faction to another. Persons and personalities become more critical and issues less critical to electoral success. In short, a vote for a candidate is even further disassociated from an expression of preference for any particular policy or collection of policies.

Incompetence in Ascertaining Citizens' Wishes. Finally, party competition on policy issues can put control over policy into the hands of the voter only to the degree that the parties correctly ascertain voters' attitudes and wishes, and succeed in formulating attractive policy packages. As new issues have entered into American politics—the various liberation movements, and energy and environmental issues, for example—American political parties have not greatly changed their appeals. For reasons of motivation and ideology, as well as of information and competence, the parties have found it difficult to understand and respond to the new groupings among voters.[17]

WHICH MAJORITY?

A final set of complications in voter control arises from discrepancies among different kinds of majorities. If policy satisfies one kind of majority, it frustrates another. Consider three different majorities:

1. *A majority opinion or vote in favor of a policy at a particular time:* for example, a majority preference for health insurance.
2. *A majority opinion or vote in favor of a group of officials:* for example, a majority preference for a Conservative rather than a Labour prime minister and cabinet. Whether or not a majority opinion supports any particular policy pursued by the prime minister and cabinet is irrelevant to this concept of majority.
3. *A legislative majority* in a system in which, through proportional representation, each group of like-minded voters chooses its representatives.

Insofar as American government can be called majoritarian at all, it operates in large part through the first kind of majority. The British system operates in large part through the second, and continental Western European multiparty systems through the third. In the third, members of parliament, each representing some such group as the Catholics, urban working-class, middle class, or peasants, find themselves in parliament not because a majority chose them but because various unified minorities did so. Parliament chooses those policies agreed to by a majority of representatives of minorities.[18] Ordinarily a policy can satisfy any one of these majorities only by not satisfying the others. Anyone who believes that democracy provides for majority control over policy must acknowledge that at best it satisfies only a particular kind of majority at the expense of the others.

---

[17]Warren E. Miller and Teresa E. Levitan, *Leadership and Change* (Cambridge, Mass.: Winthrop Publishers, 1976).

[18]A good brief description of the variety of party systems is in Gabriel Almond, ed., *Comparative Politics Today* (Boston: Little, Brown & Co., 1974), pp. 88–112.

CHAPTER THIRTEEN

FORMING THE AGENDA

If all people want warmth, security, love, and food, their political demands still will vary greatly because there are innumerable ways to satisfy these basic wants. There exist no bedrock fixed political wants or preferences; all are acquired from society and, for every individual, depend on society: what it teaches, asks, and offers.

The desire for food, for example, may be connected to a variety of possible political demands: for lower food prices, for food stamps or other subsidies, for programs to increase farm acreage, for socialized agriculture, or for food imports. The connection made between the need for food on the one hand, and political demands on the other, depends on what people want to eat, the customary mechanisms for producing and distributing it, and opinions or judgments about ways of improving these mechanisms. A political demand, for example, for lower food prices will arise only in a society in which people buy and sell food.[1]

Political demands or wants also depend on any one citizen's or policy maker's appraisal of what other people want from policy making. Any one participant in the play of power usually takes positions that seem feasible in the light of public opinion or of prospects for finding allies. The participant, for example, ordinarily would endorse a minimum guaranteed income policy only when he or she thinks that others in the play of power have come, or will shortly come, to the same opinion.

A policy-making system itself has a great effect on the very aspirations, opinions, and attitudes to which policy responds. It does not oper-

---

[1]We cannot even identify our self-interest independently of our roles in the political system. R. A. Bauer, I. de Sola Pool, and L. A. Dexter, *American Business and Public Policy* (New York: Atherton Press, 1963), pp. 127–43, 472–75.

ate as a kind of machine into which people feed their wants or needs and out of which come policy decisions to satisfy them. The machine itself manufactures wants or needs. Molding the aspirations of citizens, it brings some issues to the agenda and discards others, puts some policies but not others before citizens or policy makers for choice and forms the opinions that will decide these choices. Older democratic theory made much of the merits of representative government and democracy as systems for educating the masses, for raising their political aspiration and competence so that they could both form an appropriate agenda and act intelligently on it.[2] Newer democratic theory sometimes neglects these aspects of democracy.

CIRCULARITY IN POLICY MAKING

An allegation about the market system, made popular by John Kenneth Galbraith, holds that consumers only weakly control the economy. Through sales promotion, businesses induce consumers to buy what they want them to buy. To the extent that consumers are controlled, their own control over what they buy becomes part of a circular process: the market produces what they demand, but they demand only what the market produces.

Whether the allegation is true or not, a relevant question for us is: Does a similar circularity develop in democratic politics? In the democratic play of power even if citizens get what they want (which we have seen they do only partially on most issues), on some or many issues do they ask only for what their leaders have taught or indoctrinated them to want? Traditionally liberal democrats have assumed that competition among leaders protects the citizen from indoctrination at their hands. Educated by information and advice from their competing leaders, the citizen can make a relatively enlightened choice among policies. Only if information and advice were to come entirely from one group of like-minded leaders would the citizen become indoctrinated rather than enlightened.

Obviously leaders disagree on countless issues, and citizens benefit from debate among them. Anyone can think of dozens or hundreds of issues on which disagreement is undeniable both between parties and among members of the same party. Questions remain. On certain important issues do leaders agree? On those issues do they indoctrinate citizens, making democratic control circular or short-circuited? For convenience, let us call certain fundamental issues and policies concern-

---

[2]How agendas are formed is now being studied by a growing number of political scientists. See, for example, Roger W. Cobb and Charles D. Elder, *Participation in American Politics* (Baltimore: Johns Hopkins University Press, 1972).

ing the basic structure of the system *primary* and call the countless ordinary issues on which conflict is apparent *secondary*. The question, then, is whether on primary issues leaders agree and indoctrinate citizens.

EVIDENCE OF OPINION HOMOGENEITY AND OF INDOCTRINATION

Homogeneity

In American society there exists, not simply among leaders but throughout the society, a high degree of agreement on a number of basic issues pertaining to the structure of the society and the rules of the play of power. Americans overwhelmingly agree on the desirability of a presidential rather than a parliamentary system, or at least on their disinclination to make a change. They also largely agree on maintaining private enterprise, on a relatively high degree of corporate autonomy, and on private property. They also oppose any but very gradual (if even that) redistribution of wealth. Obviously they disagree on many connected secondary issues—for example, on how far corporations should be required to go in environmental cleanup. But their agreement on certain basic institutional or structural positions seems solid.

As a result of this degree of homogeneity of opinion on primary issues, some possible alternative policies never appear on the policy-making agenda. Political leaders neither debate nor propose action, for example, on the elimination of private property in production or in replacing the president with a prime minister. That on certain issues people overwhelmingly agree and consequently restrict the policy-making agenda, has greatly impressed many political scientists. Many have taken the position that democracy survives only because agreement on certain fundamentals keeps certain divisive issues off the agenda.[3]

Indoctrination as Cause

One can shrug off opinion homogeneity on primary issues as no more than the cohesion of thought that develops in any culture. Agreement on morals and aesthetics as well as on politics binds a collection of people together into a culture, society, or nation. That may be true. But again the questions: Just how is this homogeneity achieved? And does it undercut popular control by inducing citizens to demand in politics only a narrow range of policies endorsed by their leaders? The naturalness of homogeneity of opinion does not deny either that it has sources or that it may render popular control to a significant degree circular.

[3]A brief summary of views on the need for consensus is in Jack Walker, "A Critique of the Elitist Theory of Democracy," *American Political Science Review,* 50 (June 1966), p. 286.

On another ground one might doubt that homogeneity originates in indoctrination. One might suggest that all people have the same needs or wants, and if left free to vote and speak as they wish, all will vote and speak for roughly the same things. Such a view confuses basic wants or needs with policy choices. People everywhere do indeed need food, protection against the elements, and sociability; biological similarity produces common preferences at that level of generality. We have just noted that the complexities of history, culture, technology, and politics create countless different ways of satisfying these wants. If people agree on policy, it is because they somehow have been taught or indoctrinated to agree. In education policy, for example, a society's choice of public schools over family tutors, or of private over public schools, or of occupational over liberal arts programs represents a complex socially or culturally determined choice, not a direct response to human biology.

Some democratic theorists perhaps have misled us by talking about political preferences as though a citizen's opinion in favor of energy conservation was somehow like a preference to eat when hungry. Policy choices can hardly be called preferences. Along with elements of preference, they contain large elements of empirical belief, practical judgment, and ethical conviction. When a citizen favors nuclear power generation, he or she comes to that conclusion only through an intricate variety of considerations. They include beliefs as to fact, guesses or predictions about future events, hypotheses, however crude, about causes and effects, attitudes and values, and complex even if clumsy and inaccurate calculations that try to bring all the elements of the problem to one final synthesis and decision. The citizen ends up with a disposition to believe or act in a particular way, a volition. It is far removed from what are properly called preferences.

If all that is true, then it follows that if citizens tend to agree on primary political issues, it is because they somehow have learned to believe much the same facts, to make roughly the same guesses about future events, to formulate the same crude hypotheses, to hold to the same attitudes and values, and to weigh all these considerations together in much the same way. We must therefore identify a learning process that accounts for the similarities.

To find it, we must consider further the kind of political issues on which people tend to have the same opinion. One is that they do not want to assault many of the privileges of the wealthy and of the most favored strata or classes in society, including ownership of wealth itself. When universal male suffrage was granted in England, Karl Marx confidently predicted that the masses of working people would use their votes to dismantle the structure of wealth and privilege under which they suffered great deprivation. That they did not do so, that no body of citizens in any democracy has done so, represents, from some points of view, an extraordinary fact. Somehow people have learned not to attack wealth and privilege.[4]

Who or what taught such a lesson—the people's own insight into the merits of wealth and privilege? Some observers would argue that the great mass of people understands the need for an elite of wealth and privilege, that they perpetuate a concentration of wealth, not because they cannot clearly perceive their own interests, but because they perceive their own dependence on an elite of wealth. This argument hardly holds water. If it were true that the great mass of voters benefited from an elite of wealth and privilege, (for purposes of the argument we can grant the possibility), it seems inconceivable that voters in all the democracies, historical and contemporary, could know this to be true. If they all believed it, their agreement must be explained by some process of social indoctrination, not by their insight into reasonably well proven fact.

If people do not know the earth is round, then we can expect them to disagree on its shape. If they all agree that it is flat, we can infer that they somehow have been indoctrinated. Similarly, if they do not *know* the earth is round, their agreement on its roundness must be traced to some indoctrination. The actual shape of the world is irrelevant as an explanation of their agreement.

That no democracy has put on its agenda a major frontal assault on wealth and its attendant privileges is an historical fact of pivotal importance, for in an open-minded exploration of possible policies concerning the wealthy, the probability that some democracy would attempt such an attack is extremely high. Some democratic governments—Sweden, for example—have pushed modest attacks on inequality further than others have. Some European socialist parties have declared their intention to go beyond that to a major assault on inequality. But on winning power they have not in fact followed through. That none follows through approaches zero probability, except on the assumption of a powerful uniform social indoctrination.

Another illustrative policy issue also suggests indoctrination. Except perhaps as a temporary war measure, no democracy has ever put on its agenda a policy of central planning and displacement of the market system. Nor has most of the citizenry of a democracy ever agreed on such a policy. Although all governments continue to manipulate the boundaries between the central direction of the economy and the market system, in not a single one has citizen opinion urged relatively broad and comprehensive central planning to displace the market. Informed and thoughtful

---

[4]On whether working-class Americans know their own interests, see John Howard, "Public Policy and the White Working Class," in *The Use and Abuse of Social Science*, 2nd ed., ed. Louis Horowitz (New Brunswick, N.J.: Transaction Books, 1975).

intellectuals write books and articles arguing over its feasibility; no one can say that everyone *knows* it cannot work. Again, therefore, the uniform rejection of it by all democracies seems to require that we acknowledge social indoctrination or primary issues.

Selective Homogeneity Versus a Bias Toward the Status Quo

Homogeneity of opinion on primary issues of economic and political structure differs from a related phenomenon: the bias of societies toward the status quo. For many societies one might doubt the latter. Although many social scientists allege such a bias or note special disabilities suffered by persons seeking to alter the status quo,[5] in Western history change proceeds easily and rapidly along certain lines. In American and Eastern European societies, many people prize new forms of speech, art, and dress. Great institutional changes also occur with little evidence of resistance: for example, the bureaucratization of work, of government, of education, and even of some forms of recreation. The rise of the big corporation itself represents a monumental change. Not a general bias toward the status quo, but a conformity of opinion only on certain issues appears to operate in these societies. Although endorsing such fundamental changes as have been favored by corporate and other bureaucratic forms of social organization, attitudes remain selectively hostile to challenges to the existing distribution of wealth and challenges to corporate prerogatives. The pattern of indoctrinated belief supports wealth and business, but not all elements of the status quo.

Sources of Indoctrination

Those people most favored by any existing social system will wish to teach its virtues to those not favored. History records many successful attempts of the favored to persuade the disadvantaged to approve of their own disadvantages: for example, the medieval doctrine that heavenly pleasures await the disadvantaged—or at least those who do not in their earthly incarnations challenge the dominant earthly order—or the doctrine of the divine right of kings. In our era, favored groups or elites, elites of wealth and business, wish to persuade the citizenry to accept a concentration of wealth and its attendant privileges, corporate autonomy, and the privileged position of business—all as necessary to the citizen's welfare.

Of their capacity to persuade, earlier chapters have already provided the evidence. The "competition of ideas" that ostensibly characterizes a democracy is an unequal competition. Political persuasion, we have seen, is enormously one-sided. Although not silenced, dissident voices

---

[5]On the alleged bias toward the status quo, see Peter Bachrach and Morton Baratz, *Power and Poverty* (New York: Oxford University Press, 1970), especially p. 58.

cannot speak frequently or to the largest audiences. For all the specific reasons given in earlier chapters on business privilege, interest groups, and inequality, dissident voices cannot speak as loudly or as frequently as the voices of wealth and of business, especially on those issues on which policy makers join with business.

Even in the universities, which pride themselves on their internal competition of ideas, some ideas systematically dominate. Denying that its economics faculty had seriously attacked the American system, a recent president of Harvard declared:

> Can anyone seriously charge that these men and the others in their department are subverting the American way of life? And can one seriously charge the same of the University as a whole, taking note of its program in history, government, public administration and social relations, and its far-reaching effort in business, which is almost completely directed toward making the private enterprise system continue to work effectively and beneficially in a very difficult world.[6]

In a grossly unequal competition of ideas, the advantages of the wealthy and of business strike at the very foundation of democracy—the capacity of the citizen to analyze his or her own needs and to find policies for meeting them.

As noted before, neither the wealthy nor business leadership constitutes a wholly homogenous opinion group, nor do they always agree with each other. Only on primary issues do they largely agree among themselves and with each other. Only on primary issues about the very structure of the political-economic system do they carry the same message to the citizen.

On primary issues of economic and political structure, the policy-making elite joins in the same message. For the reasons given in chapter 9 on the privileged position of business, policy makers cannot win from business the performance needed for jobs, stability, and growth while simultaneously attacking the foundations of the economic order. They try to make an existing system work rather than greatly reform it. Hardly less so than business people do political leaders endorse the "American Way."

In the elite of knowledgeables are many policy makers and business employees. If any of the knowledgeables offer a potential for dissent from the uniformity of elite opinion on primary issues, it must be sought in a subgroup of them who are relatively independent of business and government: scholars, teachers, journalists, writers, or other intellectuals speaking independently on economics and politics. Other elites in fact

---

[6]Nathan M. Pusey, *The Age of The Scholar* (Cambridge, Mass.: Harvard University Press, 1963), p. 171.

often single out such independent members of the subgroup as danger-ously dissident. But they are only a small number. The publications of the subgroup, like the testimony of the Harvard president, indicate that only a few of them raise questions challenging the homogeneity we have described. Those who do so are an extremely small group, even smaller in the United States than in Western Europe, whose identification as a political elite would have to rest on the principle that the pen is eventually mightier than the sword. In the very long run, the dissidents in such a subgroup presumably change political and economic systems. They influ-ence day-to-day policy making very little.

DUAL BLOCKAGE

We now set the conclusion of this chapter alongside earlier conclusions about the looseness of popular control in a democratic system. On the usual issues of politics, we have seen many obstacles impede effective citizen control over policy making, obstacles identified chapter by chap-ter. To an already long list of obstacles emerging in the description of the play of power, the discussion of inequality and of imprecision in voting added more. Only on a few issues that we call primary do govern-ments consistently give citizens what they say they want. On these pri-mary issues, however, citizens appear to be indoctrinated to a significant degree so that they ask for what leadership already wishes to give them. On the primary issues, popular control therefore becomes to some sig-nificant degree circular. An indoctrinated citizenry does not put these troublesome issues on the agenda. No one acts on them. Even specula-tion on radical new forms of social organization is left to poets, profes-sors, utopian novelists, essayists, and writers of comic strips.

In short, popular control is either loose or circular, one ailment afflicting policy making on secondary issues, the other afflicting policy on primary issues. Either way, popular control is weak.

POSTSCRIPT

In the opening chapters, we found various reasons why analysis of policy problems reaches limits beyond which it cannot go and, conversely, why political interaction becomes necessary to policy making. Among these, two stand out: limited human cognitive capacity and conflicts over goals, values, and criteria.

Because policies consequently follow from political interactions rather than from analytical conclusions, the process does not correspond to conventionally conceived rational problem solving, which is an intellectual process. Even if an observer approves of the outcome, he can say the process is rational only if he means no more than that it produces what he approves of. As for the outcome as distinct from process, if he calls it rational, he again ordinarily means no more than that he approves.

Instead of reaching "solutions" that can be judged by standards of rationality, policy making reaches settlements, reconciliations, adjustments, and agreements that one can evaluate only inconclusively by such standards as fairness, acceptability, openness to reconsideration and responsiveness to a variety of interests. And analysis in large part is transformed from an evaluative technique into a method of exerting influence, control and power which we call partisan analysis.

Some democratic theorists have seen democratic policy-making processes as a search for truth, hence have tried to reconcile democratic policy making with the scientific vision of policy making discussed in chapter 5. But on the whole, democratic theory has tended to discredit the idea that policy making constitutes or accomplishes a search for truth, for correct policies, or for rationality in politics. Instead, it proposes another test of good policy: that it is willed, chosen, or preferred, with the choice indicated ultimately by how people vote among candidates.

Given the prestige of science and rationality in the contemporary world, democratic skepticism about the scientific vision of policy making creates a continuing unease in the democracies as to what citizens should expect of politicians, policy makers, and themselves.

Democratic criteria for good policy making and good outcomes do not necessarily include criteria like fairness, openness to reconsideration, and responsiveness to a wide array of interests. Like these criteria, however, democratic criteria judge process rather than result, as is appropriate for a predominately interactive or political rather than intellectual process. Right policies are those that emerge from right processes, and right processes are those in which citizens choose for themselves, no matter how foolishly.

We have seen that despite a powerful democratic tradition, policy making in the United States in fact does not respond well to popular control. Nor does it easily meet other standards. Some observers claim that it at least accommodates a variety of sources of fresh information and analysis, that it feeds on new ideas. Indeed it does. That might count as one of American policy making's greatest strengths. But our analysis of indoctrination indicates a limit. Other observers claim that in the democracies everyone can speak his or her mind and exert some influence. Again, we can accept the claim—up to a point. Political inequality silences many citizens. Other observers claim that participants in the play of power play in a fair competition in that all participants can use basically the same methods. In the face of the privileged position of business, this claim looks dubious.

Others claim only that democratic rules disperse influence, control, and power, in consequence of which many interests influence policy making, even if not fairly or equally. That important claim has some validity, but within limits set by indoctrination. A stronger claim than any of these may be that democratic policy making keeps the social peace. Sufficiently flexible, sufficiently open, and sufficiently given to endless reconsideration of policies, it encourages an eternal hopefulness even among the disadvantaged. Few people, consequently, try civil disorder or rebellion.

We noted that an older justification for democracy was that it protected our liberties, not that it gave the public control over policy making. For some people, neither that justification nor any of the others just listed any longer suffices. For them, the principal claim to be made for democracy is that it offers a potential, yet to be tapped, for popular control over policy.

If so, the realization of that potential presumably will not come easily. The machinery of policy making, we have seen, creaks with its complexities. Yet people must move that very machinery in order to rebuild it, that is, to alter the policy-making process so that the democratic potential can be realized. Standing in the way are both misapprehensions and genuine obstacles.

Many people do not understand that their fellow citizens are a principal obstacle to their achieving an influence on policy. In recent years many proponents of educational reform, new foreign policies, liberation movements, and other causes on the frontiers of public policy come to a stop, not simply because elites stand in their way but because millions of their equally empowered fellow citizens also do. To move them is a massive and improbable undertaking. As we noted before, democracy plays a cruel joke. It gives some power to the citizen, but it also gives power to all other citizens. For any one person, consequently, most of his fellow citizens constitute barriers to having his own way.

Beyond the inertia or resistance of millions of fellow citizens, anyone who wishes to improve the policy-making process must cope with the two roadblocks: the looseness of popular control on ordinary political issues, and its degree of circularity on primary issues. These features of policy making he or she presumably wishes to correct. But everything that can be done to alter them they obstruct by now standing in the way.

To improve the policy-making process, a citizen must enter into policy making. Whether entering into it to influence a particular policy or to improve the whole process, he or she takes on a formidable task. Policy making is laborious for all persons who want to achieve more than a minimum effect. Policy making reserves the big shares of influence to those who recognize that one participates in the play of power not as a privilege but as an exceedingly demanding task or career. In the last analysis, one does not play at the play of power. One must toil at it.

TO EXPLORE FURTHER

Because the study of policy making is the study of all of politics from a particular point of view, reading on any aspects of politics will strengthen the student's understanding of policy making: for example, readings on voter behavior, the presidency, the legislature, the courts, the bureaucracy, decision making, international relations, democratic theory, authoritarianism, comparative politics, and political philosophy, among others. I shall therefore have to be highly selective—even arbitrary—in making suggestions.

I first suggest that further reading begin with the footnotes in this book. Many of them indicate further reading on topics discussed in the chapters. Other possibilities are the books in this series: for example, Herbert Kaufman's *Politics and Policies in State and Local Governments,* which discusses an area of policy making not covered in this book.

Besides the footnoted items, a selection of readings like the following discusses various aspects of policy making from many points of view. The earliest of them is Pendleton Herring, *The Politics of Democracy* (New York: Rinehart & Company, Inc., 1940; new edition, New York: W. W. Norton & Co., Inc., 1965), an extraordinarily insightful analysis of government, politics, and policy making with a richer implicit than explicit theoretical content. Worth reading for itself as well as for the light it throws on Herring's work is a review of a new edition of Herring by Avery Leiserson in *American Political Science Review,* 60 (June 1966). Herring's book can be contrasted with a carefully reasoned and highly persuasive Marxist analysis: Ralph Miliband, *The State in Capitalist Society* (New York: Basic Books Inc, Publishers, 1969), and with others who challenge the pluralism that Herring represents: among many, Frank Parkin, *Class Inequality and Political Order* (New York: Praeger Publishers, 1971), and

Kenneth Prewitt and Alan Stone, *The Ruling Elites* (New York: Harper & Row, Publishers, 1973).

Case studies of policy making now abound and are easily accessible. Among tens of dozens that might be mentioned, some of the best are: Graham T. Allison, *Essence of Decision: Explaining the Cuban Missile Crisis* (Boston: Little, Brown & Co., 1971); Daniel P. Moynihan, *Maximum Feasible Misunderstanding* (New York: The Free Press, 1969) or his *Politics of a Guaranteed Income* (New York: Random House, 1973); Alexander George and others, *The Limits of Coercive Diplomacy* (Boston: Little, Brown & Co., 1971); Robert Engler, *The Politics of Oil* (New York: Macmillan Co., 1961); and Albert O. Hirschman, *Journeys Toward Progress: Studies of Economic Policy-Making in Latin America* (New York: Twentieth Century Fund, 1963).

Broader than case studies yet empirically rich are Grant McConnell, *Private Power and American Democracy* (New York: Alfred A. Knopf, Inc., 1967), and James L. Sundquist's historically oriented *Politics and Policy Making* (Washington, D.C.: Brookings Institution, 1968).

One might stretch his or her mind to see what can be extracted about policy making from some of the classics of political philosophy. In Jean Jacques Rousseau's *Social Contract,* for example, the concept of the general will clarifies political socialization, majority rule, consensus, and the role of analysis as an alternative to political interaction.

INDEX